The Vocation of the
Christian Scholar

248.88
H893 v

13.50

The Vocation of the Christian Scholar

HOW CHRISTIAN FAITH CAN SUSTAIN
THE LIFE OF THE MIND

• •

Revised Edition

Richard T. Hughes

William B. Eerdmans Publishing Company
Grand Rapids, Michigan / Cambridge, U.K.

Much of the material in this volume first appeared under the title
How Christian Faith Can Sustain the Life of the Mind (Eerdmans: 2001).

This edition © 2005 Wm. B. Eerdmans Publishing Co.
All rights reserved

Wm. B. Eerdmans Publishing Co.
255 Jefferson Ave. S.E., Grand Rapids, Michigan 49503 /
P.O. Box 163, Cambridge CB3 9PU U.K.

Printed in the United States of America

10 09 08 07 06 05   7 6 5 4 3 2 1

ISBN 0-8028-2915-5

www.eerdmans.com

For Rodney J. Sawatsky

(1943-2004)

Christian scholar, dear friend, and stimulating partner in conversation

who consistently expanded and clarified my vision and

whose lifelong embrace of paradox and ambiguity

offered me an exemplary model

of faith, hope, and love.

Contents

Foreword

A PATIENT REVOLUTION IS TAKING PLACE IN A MAJOR SECTOR of American higher education. Quite a number of colleges and universities associated with Christian denominations are taking a fresh look at their relationship with those bodies and, accordingly, their responsibilities to them.

For several decades now, many of the schools in that sector thought of as "progressive" have distanced themselves from confessional faith in the insistent interest of making adaptation to modern worldviews. Such colleges, especially their faculties, have judged that to be the responsible course of action — or at least such was their intention when modern discoveries and formulations in the sciences and the humanities emphatically mapped that out as the high road. Truth be told, the intellectual work done on those campuses became virtually indistinguishable from what prevailed at state universities. It is not amiss to suggest that most students in those institutions had no reason to reckon that theirs was a Presbyterian or Methodist or Lutheran college.

Another cluster of church-related colleges, the "evangelical" ones, also tended to live out of reaction. In response to the rush of so many churches and their colleges to accommodate their academic life to what was happening on the leading edge of work in the disciplines, these evangelicals tended to take cover, to stake their identity on being different, sometimes defiantly so. They achieved enthusiastic approval from their supporters but placed themselves beyond the range of interest and respect of the majority culture in the nation.

When these two groupings of church-supported purveyors of higher learning are added together, they total a very high proportion of American private institutions generally and Christian ones in particular. "Modern" or "secular" modes of thought had largely come to power, as reflected by the two patterns of adoption and rejection.

Richard Hughes's book belongs to a growing list of substantial reflections on this condition and what church-related colleges and universities are beginning to do about dealing with it, and may be encouraged to do further. This study achieves its distinctiveness through its theological orientation. Setting a little historical context may enable us to clarify that distinctiveness.

Colonial America's colleges were founded by Christians and existed in part to serve the direct purposes of the churches: training ministers and educating laymen. Much of the same animation obtained in the early decades of the population's westward movement. The number of such colleges planted in Pennsylvania, Ohio, Indiana, Illinois, and other states is astonishing. Of course, many of them persist, even flourish; the lot of them make up an impressive percentage of the nation's high-quality liberal arts institutions in our own time.

Along the way, a transformation occurred. State-sponsored universities emerged and over time came to claim the majority of students and funding resources to educate Americans. Accompanying that development, in fact, in large part fueling it, was the rise to dominance of secular perspectives, generally classifiable as heirs of the Enlightenment outlook on learning (but without sensitively defining that movement of early modern Europe as Hughes shows Mead and Bellah to have done). The power of these secular perspectives is exemplified by the tendency of church-founded colleges to adopt an outlook and values in sync with a secular worldview. This they often did quite uncritically. They seem hardly to have considered whether they were surrendering something of value in the process of keeping up with the times and gaining reputability. How else could intellectually progressive educators function? Many, however, did retain some degree of connection to their historic denominational ties. Moreover, attention to values and excellence in teaching — students, not merely subjects — remained a trademark of those schools.

Yet, the "idea of a Christian university" enjoyed little aggressive support and generated little creative reflection on what Christian higher education is or might be. Even some Catholic colleges were overtaken by this secular juggernaut, with not very much resistance from ecclesiastical leadership. Excellence in this modern era was thought simply to be synonymous with the up-to-date, "enlightened" perspectives, that is, the secular ideal.

An "evangelical resurgence" that began after the Second World War attained a significant social standing by the 1970s. To the surprise of many, conservative Protestantism, shedding much of its isolationism and defensiveness, was beginning to devote serious attention to higher education. An outsider to this sector of American religious life might have assumed that its colleges, academies, and seminaries would carry on with business as usual by being somewhat or much withdrawn from secular society, given to protecting their young from "modernism" (not the same as "modernity," incidentally). The general supposition, especially to any who were misinformed — and even given to prejudging — seems to have been that we could expect little from these Christians in the way of boldly free and risk-filled inquiry into the life of the mind.

How different the reality is today from such suppositions. Witness the work of scholars like George Marsden, Nathan Hatch, and Mark Noll; the creative and courageous leadership of such colleges as Calvin, Wheaton, and Messiah; and the stimulating hard-nosed intellectual contributions of *Books and Culture, Fides et Historia,* and other journals. Those achievements have extended far beyond the traditional evangelical orbit — itself large and diverse — to make an impact on many sectors of the American Christian community, even on American intellectual life at large. Other colleges and universities have joined the leadership ranks of this new era in Christian higher education, including Notre Dame (Catholic), Valparaiso (Lutheran), Baylor (Southern Baptist), and now Pepperdine (Churches of Christ), to mention only some of the more visible.

Richard Hughes of the last-mentioned institution essays here to equip this regeneration and redirection with an outline of several theological themes, all of them ingredients in the belief systems of representative Christian interpretations. He does so by drawing upon Reformed, Catholic, Mennonite, and Lutheran thought heritages. Each item in the outline he esteems as authentically Christian and supportive of "the life of the mind." Perhaps he holds in highest regard the device of paradox; it has the merit of subverting authoritarianism and absolutism while also fostering critical inquiry.

The time seems to have come for replacing the bifurcation of reality into Nature and Spirit (associated with the work of Kant) with an affirmation of the unity and integrity of these realities. Hughes's contribution to this development is constructive and joins that of others who have a passion for intellectual exploration and the transmission of knowledge to students (of all ages). As a person of the church, he lives with the conviction that Christian colleges and universities are commissioned to practice that integrity — with hard labor and sensitivity. He offers these pages with that calling in mind.

These extensive efforts to renew Christian perspectives, values, and goals to Christian higher education have become a significant force. They are being heard and their claims considered even by a number of scholars in public institutions. (I know that as one who has spent almost his entire career teaching in state universities.)

Indeed, this book addresses not only those Christian scholars who practice their craft in the context of Christian institutions of higher learning but also those Christian scholars who practice their craft in private and state-supported institutions. And the message is the same in both instances: it is possible to cultivate the highest level of scholarship, not in spite of one's Christian commitments but precisely because of those commitments.

Much remains to be done, of course. One hopes that the studious approaches to the cause taken between 1930 and 1960 or so by the Moberly-Coleman-Nash school of thought, the work of the Kent and Danforth programs, and the journal *The Christian Scholar* will be resumed in forms that are pertinent to our situation. These could be companion efforts to what the Lilly Endowment, numerous colleges and publications, and an impressive cadre of thinkers are accomplishing today. This book, and the tireless labors of its author in writing and speaking, contributes to this ongoing task.

SAMUEL S. HILL
University of Florida

xiii

Preface to the Revised Edition:
THE VOCATION OF THE CHRISTIAN SCHOLAR

I HAVE OFTEN THOUGHT THAT THE BOOK WE CALLED IN ITS first edition *How Christian Faith Can Sustain the Life of the Mind*[1] could just as well have been called *The Vocation of the Christian Scholar*. Now, in this second edition, we have done just that.

To focus the title of the book on the theme of vocation is altogether appropriate since, while this book is in certain ways theoretical, it is also profoundly autobiographical. It grows, after all, from my own personal struggle to define for myself what it means to embrace the vocation of a Christian scholar. In this preface to the second edition, therefore, I want to bring to light the vocational dimensions of this text and to make explicit what is only implicit in the first edition, namely, my own personal quest for vocational integrity.

This second edition also contains an exploration of another aspect of vocation, namely, "the vocation of a Christian college," the theme of chapter seven. I hope the reflections contained in this preface and chapter, both of them new to this text, will encourage readers to explore comparable themes in their own personal journeys and in the journeys of their institutions.

---

1. Richard T. Hughes, *How Christian Faith Can Sustain the Life of the Mind* (Grand Rapids: Eerdmans, 2001).

The Paradoxical Calling of the Christian Scholar

Many years ago, when I was a graduate student at the University of Iowa, I read a slender little book that would have a far-reaching impact on the way I think even now about my life and my vocation. Written by the influential Harvard psychologist Gordon W. Allport, the book was entitled, simply, *Becoming.*

There, Allport argued that the healthy personality is one that is "meaningfully linked to the whole of Being."[2] While it is doubtful that we can link ourselves to "the whole of Being," this concept nonetheless suggests that if we have any hope of becoming psychologically healthy human beings, we must integrate every aspect of our lives around a core identity that stands at the center of our self-understanding. It simply will not do for one dimension of my life to run in one direction while other dimensions of my life run in radically different directions, especially if no one dimension is consistent with any other.

This book takes its point of departure from the recognition that no one in contemporary American society is more likely to lead a fundamentally fragmented life than a Christian who is also a scholar. Why? Because the Christian faith and the academy seem to operate from such radically different premises, and both demand our allegiance. Jesus said, "I am *the* way, *the* truth, and *the* life. No one comes to the Father but by me." On the other hand, the academy encourages us to take seriously the many competing voices that claim to be voices of truth. No wonder that Tertullian pressed the question, "What has Athens to do with Jerusalem?"

Many Christian scholars would like to sing the songs of Zion in this strange and alien land, but seldom open their mouths because the songs they wish to sing and the land they inhabit seem so completely at odds in terms of fundamental presuppositions. They re-

---

2. Gordon W. Allport, *Becoming: Basic Considerations for a Psychology of Personality* (New Haven: Yale University Press, 1955), p. 94.

solve this dilemma, therefore, in the easiest way they know how: They are Christians on Sunday and scholars on Monday, and never the twain shall meet. By leading such radically fragmented lives, they cripple their effectiveness as Christians, as scholars, and as human beings.

This book seeks to address this dilemma. It asks the simple question, "How can I bring my identity as a Christian and my identity as a scholar and a teacher into sync with one another, and thereby embrace a holistic and consistent vocation?" And it addresses that question by asking another: "How can Christian faith sustain the life of the mind?"

If this description helps us understand, at least at a very basic level, what this book is and what it seeks to do, it might be helpful to also describe what this book is *not*. I can address that question most effectively by contrasting this book with another text that, at least on the surface of things, appears to raise comparable questions and issues. That other book is George Marsden's *The Outrageous Idea of Christian Scholarship*.[3]

The most fundamental difference between these two books is this: If Marsden explores the *ideal* of "Christian *scholarship*," my concern is to explore the *vocation* of the Christian *scholar*. If Marsden asks about the product, I ask about the person who creates the product. I respect and honor the inquiry that Marsden has undertaken, but his question is not the question that I place front and center.

In fact, I am not nearly so concerned to produce "Christian scholarship" as I am to make certain that I function as a scholar who is also a Christian, and as a Christian who is also a scholar, whose scholarship is informed by my Christian commitments and whose Christian faith is enhanced by serious scholarship.

In fact, it is not always clear to me what might qualify as "Chris-

---

3. George M. Marsden, *The Outrageous Idea of Christian Scholarship* (New York: Oxford University Press, 1997).

tian scholarship." But it is clear to me what it means to serve as a "Christian scholar."

As I note later in this text, Professor Paul Griffiths of the University of Chicago Divinity School once remarked that "one is a Christian scholar if one understands one's work to be based upon and framed by and always in the service of one's identity as a Christian."[4] In the same vein, Madeleine L'Engle once told a student who wished to become a "Christian writer" that "if she is truly and deeply a Christian, what she writes is going to be Christian, whether she mentions Jesus or not. And if she is not, in the most profound sense, Christian, then what she writes is not going to be Christian, no matter how many times she invokes the name of the Lord."[5]

The fundamental question here is the question of vocation, for the question of vocation is finally a question of who we are, really, deep down inside — the point at which we find our deepest meaning, our deepest gladness, and our deepest joy. For this reason, the question of the vocation of the Christian scholar always takes precedence over the question of Christian scholarship.

The question of vocation is simply this: do we have an identity that stands at the core of our being, an identity that informs every other aspect of our lives and around which every other aspect of our lives can be integrated?

To frame the question in this way, however, does not altogether resolve our dilemma. For the plain fact is, those of us who are both Christians and scholars will inevitably live in the midst of a deep and inescapable paradox. As Christians, we are committed to a highly particularistic tradition. Yet, as scholars, we are also committed to a radical search for truth that simultaneously embraces particularity and ambiguity, knowing and not knowing, affirmation and investi-

---

4. Paul Griffiths in a question-and-answer session following his lecture, "Seeking Egyptian Gold," at Lilly Fellows Program meeting, Valparaiso University, October 8, 1999.

5. Madeleine L'Engle, *Walking on Water: Reflections on Faith and Art* (Wheaton, Ill.: Harold Shaw Publishers, 1980), pp. 121-22.

gation. We are called to honor our Christian faith, but we are also called to take seriously the diversity of perspectives that abound in the modern academy. It is not our job to trump those perspectives with our Christian convictions. Instead, we are called to engage those perspectives, really engage them, and bring them into dialogue with the Christian faith.

It seems obvious, then, that if we seek to integrate every aspect of our lives around a core identity that stands at the center of our self-understanding, that core identity must itself be framed by a paradoxical vision. To make this point another way, the vocation of the Christian scholar must itself be built on paradox, simply because we cannot escape the paradox that frames our work and our calling.

The truth is, the Christian scholar can find the basis for a paradoxical self-understanding very near at hand, simply because the notion of paradox stands at the very core of the Christian message. We find paradox, for example, in the idea of the incarnation — the infinite God of the universe who takes on the form of human flesh and who enters this world amidst cows and pigs in a lowly manger. We also find paradox at the core of the Christian gospel — we are inescapably sinners from first to last, but at the very same time, God calls us righteous, leading Luther to exclaim, *simul justus et peccator* — "simultaneously justified and a sinner." And the notion of paradox runs through virtually all the teachings of Jesus. We must lose ourselves to find ourselves, he says. We must die in order to live. We can only be first by being last.

Over the years, this gospel, with its profoundly paradoxical message, has become the basis for my own sense of identity and vocation. To help readers of this book understand how this came to be, I now share the story of my own journey toward vocational wholeness and integrity.

My Journey toward Vocational Integrity

When one is raised in a religious tradition that claims to be the one true church outside of which there can be no salvation, one takes that tradition seriously. Indeed, one can do no other. And when that tradition insists on perfection — both moral perfection and religious perfection — and when as an adolescent one continually falls short of those expectations, the psychic pressure is palpable. This is the way my story begins, for I was raised in the Church of Christ at a time before the Church of Christ at large either heard or proclaimed the good news of God's grace.

For a very long time, therefore, I understood the gospel not in terms of grace and redemption, but in terms of obligation, of perseverance, of finding and possessing the truth, and of living according to God's decrees. This understanding of the gospel is a heavy burden for anyone to bear, especially an adolescent.

As an eleven- and twelve-year-old boy, I had to walk to my elementary school in San Angelo, Texas, and to reach the school, I had to cross a very busy thoroughfare. It occurred to me every day that in the process of crossing that street, I could easily be killed. But I also reminded myself every day that if, per chance, I was struck by a car, I had to remember to pray before I expired, "Lord, forgive me for all those sins, for smoking all those cigarettes, for looking at all those pretty girls, for telling those dirty jokes, for saying those nasty words, and for failing to keep my mind on Jesus when I last took communion."

These were my "besetting sins" when I was eleven and twelve years old. I wanted to clean up my act, but found it almost impossible to do so. As a result, I nurtured a substantial load of guilt. But I also nurtured the belief that if I breathed that prayer of contrition before I died, I would no doubt be welcomed into the pearly gates. But if I forgot to pray and I died with my sins unforgiven, I would surely burn in hell for an eternity.

In those days, I obviously had no meaningful understanding of the gospel at all. For me, the gospel meant that one was in a state of grace following a prayer, but out of grace following the very next sin or sinful thought.

The guilt I experienced, coupled with my conviction that my church was the one true church outside of which there could be no salvation, finally drove me to accomplish two tasks. The first was the task of self-understanding. I knew I could never understand myself unless I understood the religious tradition that had formed and shaped me. This is precisely why I undertook the study of Christian history and why I finally felt driven to make that study both my vocation and my career. This is also why I have devoted so much of my career to researching and writing the history of the Churches of Christ.

Discovering Justification by Grace through Faith

My second task was to find some way to escape the burden of perfectionism that was so much a part of my religious upbringing. My mother freed me to address this task when I was probably a junior in high school. In those days, I brought my high school buddies home after school so that I could show them a set of filmstrips designed to convert them to the Church of Christ. My friends were mainly Baptists, Methodists, and Presbyterians.

One day my mother said to me, "Son, if you want to convert your friends to the Church of Christ, that's fine with me. However, if you discover that they're right and you're wrong, then you need to be the one who is willing to make the change." Her comment that day freed me to admit that I could be wrong, an admission I have since come to believe is the first step toward hearing — really hearing — the gospel of grace.

But it wasn't until I was a sophomore in college that I really heard the gospel of grace for the very first time. This wondrous event occurred in the midst of a course on the book of Romans in 1962.

The professor was lecturing on Romans 8:1: "Therefore, there is now no condemnation for those who are in Christ Jesus."

When the teacher read these words, he waxed warm and eloquent. In truth, he began to preach. "No one," he said, as he leaned into the lectern toward the students, "No one can possibly be good enough, smart enough, or right enough to earn or deserve salvation. We are saved," he affirmed, "not because we are good or right or perfect, but only through the unmerited grace and favor of God who loves and accepts us in spite of our sin and rebellion. Salvation is the gift of God's infinite love and grace."

For me, this message was revolutionary, and I was stunned by what I heard. My professor's words set me on the road toward freedom — freedom from self-reliance, freedom from perfectionism, and freedom from the compulsion always to be right.

Then, a few years later, at the University of Iowa, one of my teachers — Professor George Forell — made explicit what had been only implicit before. In a class on "The Theology of Martin Luther," Forell explained how for Luther, the gospel is fundamentally a paradoxical message. For Luther, Forell explained, the heart of the gospel lies in the fact that, as Christians, we never cease to be redeemed, though we never cease to be sinners. Sinful and redeemed simultaneously, Forell explained. What a paradox! *Simul justus et peccator.*

When Luther advised his followers to "sin boldly," I now understood what he meant. I was free to embrace my humanity. I didn't need to be God and I didn't need to be perfect. But I did need to trust God's pledge that his grace was sufficient, even for someone like me.

That class for me was a conversion experience. Thanks to that class, I have felt ever since a deep connection with Martin Luther who opened for me the riches of the Christian gospel in extraordinary ways. In fact, I was so drawn to Luther and the way he framed this gospel that, in a very real sense, I became a Lutheran, at least in my heart of hearts, and it is safe to say that I have been a Lutheran in that sense from that time on. Recently, a friend of mine who wrote a history of the Lutheran Church Missouri Synod — Mary Todd — gave me a copy of her book and inscribed it, "To Richard — honorary Lutheran that you are." Deeply honored by that inscription, I felt that she knew me well.

Discovering the Meaning of Sanctification

To this point, I had escaped the burden of perfectionism by discovering the gospel of grace. But there was still more to be done. I was not prepared to leave the Churches of Christ, but I desperately wanted to find a way to translate its perfectionistic demands into categories that seemed more meaningful — and more biblical — than the legalism with which I was raised. I began to take that step as a graduate student at Abilene Christian University, for there I discovered another sixteenth-century Christian tradition — the tradition of the Anabaptists, often known as the "radicals of the Reformation."

Before my sojourn at Abilene Christian, I had never heard of the Anabaptists. Having grown up in West Texas, I knew nothing of the Mennonite tradition whatsoever. Then, during that year of graduate study at ACU, one of my teachers, Professor Everett Ferguson, placed in my hands a book that would transform my life in far-reaching ways. That book was *The Origins of Sectarian Protestantism* by Franklin H. Littell.[6] Littell argued in that book that the heart of sixteenth-century Anabaptism was the quest for the restoration of the primitive church.

The restoration of the primitive church? I resonated with that language at a very deep level since my own church — the Church of Christ — had employed this very same language to define its mission, its agenda, and indeed, its very reason for existence.

One of the principal founders of my tradition, Alexander

6. Franklin H. Littell, *The Origins of Sectarian Protestantism* (New York: Macmillan, 1964, first published in 1952 as *The Anabaptist View of the Church*).

Campbell, had argued in the early nineteenth century that the restoration of the primitive church could provide the strongest possible basis for the unity of all Christians. Ironically, the movement Campbell helped establish soon split along the lines of that original agenda. One wing of that split, the northern-based Disciples of Christ, claimed the unity motif and soon provided one of the most eloquent voices in American Christendom for ecumenical relations. The other wing of that split, the southern-based Churches of Christ, claimed the restoration motif and, for some two hundred years, has argued passionately for the recovery of the primitive church, defined by the New Testament documents. This was the tradition in which I was raised.

Frank Littell's book on Anabaptism was for me a revelation. I brought to that book the understanding of restoration that I had learned in Churches of Christ. In my tradition, we had always defined primitive Christianity in terms of forms and structures. How should the church be organized, for example? How should the sacraments be observed, and how often? How should worship be conducted? Could we discern in the biblical text a definitive "plan of salvation"? Churches of Christ argued that the Bible offered a pattern — we sometimes called it a "blueprint" — that would resolve each of these questions with abundant clarity.

But according to Littell, while the Anabaptists sought to recover the ancient church and therefore used the language of restoration, they never focused their restoration vision on forms and structures. Instead, they focused on lifestyle. If the preeminent question in my tradition was, "How can we recover the forms and structures of the ancient church?" the preeminent question for the Anabaptists was, "What does it mean to be a genuine disciple of Jesus?" And if we had found the blueprint for restoration in the picture of the early church reflected in the Book of Acts, the Anabaptists found no blueprint at all. Instead, they found both mandate and model for the task they embraced in the person of Jesus the Christ, reflected in the Gospels.

I was so struck with this contrast that I wrote my M.A. thesis comparing the way that early leaders of Churches of Christ and early leaders of sixteenth-century Anabaptism employed the category of restoration.[7] That project helped me discern another striking dimension of Anabaptism, and it was this: when Anabaptists asked what it means to be a genuine disciple of Jesus, they — like Luther — responded to that question by embracing the notion of paradox.

Granted, the Lutheran paradox and the Anabaptist paradox were of two different orders. Luther's was the paradox of justification, while the Anabaptists focused on the paradox of sanctification. Thus, if Luther embraced the *Pauline* doctrine that the Christian is simultaneously justified and a sinner, the Anabaptists embraced *Jesus'* teaching that one must die in order to live, that we find ourselves by losing ourselves, and that the first shall be last and the last shall be first. They translated this paradox into a way of life that included non-violence, the sharing of goods with those less fortunate than themselves, and the rejection of greed and self-centered ways of living.

These radicals had caught a vision of the Upside-Down Kingdom[8] — to borrow a phrase from Don Kraybill — a kingdom ruled by grace from start to finish. Thanks to the way these sixteenth-century Anabaptists witnessed in my own life, I finally began to discern what I now regard as the *fullness* of the gospel: by grace we are saved, and by grace we reach out to the neighbor.

Over the years, I have so internalized this Anabaptist vision that when I once delivered a chapel address at Goshen College, the flagship Mennonite institution, a dear friend who knows me well — Theron Schlabach — introduced me to the students as an "honorary Mennonite." So now I was both an "honorary Mennonite" and an "honorary Lutheran."

As far as a sense of vocation went, my problem now was that I

7. Richard T. Hughes, "A Critical Comparsion of the Restitution Motifs of the Campbells (1809-1830) and the Anabaptists (1524-1560)," M.A. thesis, Abilene Christian University, 1967.

8. Donald B. Kraybill, *The Upside-Down Kingdom* (Scottdale, Pa.: Herald Press, 1978).

continued as a member of Churches of Christ, whose theology I found inadequate, while I identified most fully with Luther, on the one hand, and the Anabaptists, on the other. Put another way, I found myself plunging deeper and deeper into religious and vocational schizophrenia.

Then I signed a contract to write a history of the Churches of Christ.[9] Through that project I discovered an entire side of the Churches of Christ that I had never known — a strand of my own tradition that looked much like the sixteenth-century Anabaptists, that lived by the grace of God, that sought to extend that grace to the neighbor, and that in all these ways sought to realize a vision of the Upside-Down Kingdom. Better still, this was not a minor strand but a major defining dimension of Churches of Christ in their early years — people who sold their goods and gave to the poor, people who embraced non-violence and refused to take up the sword, and people who sought to live their lives in the context of the kingdom of God where grace is the dominant reality.

That discovery was a Godsend since it allowed me to reclaim my heritage in the Churches of Christ and to find that heritage fully consistent with my commitment to the gospel of grace and to the Anabaptist vision of extending that grace to the neighbor. Better yet, since the 1960s, Churches of Christ themselves have recovered the gospel in powerful ways, and because of that recovery, I find myself more and more at home in the heritage of my youth.

This story has everything to do with my own sense of vocation, since the story of God's grace is the reason I get up every morning. Put another way, it is precisely in this story that I find my sense of selfhood and precisely here that I find meaning in my life. One should not be surprised, therefore, to learn that the theme of grace

9. Richard T. Hughes and R. L. Roberts, *The Churches of Christ* (Westport, Conn.: Greenwood Press, 2001); Richard T. Hughes, *The Churches of Christ: Student Edition* (Westport, Conn.: Praeger, 2001); and Richard T. Hughes, *Reviving the Ancient Faith: The Story of Churches of Christ in America* (Grand Rapids: Eerdmans, 1996).

— the grace God extends to me and the grace I must extend to the neighbor — informs at a fundamental level everything I teach and everything I write. Indeed, the gospel of Christ has defined my sense of vocation.

As a result, I am grateful for three Christian traditions that have led me to drink from the gospel fountain — the tradition of Martin Luther who taught me much about the grace of God, the tradition of the Anabaptists who helped me to see that the call to extend grace to the neighbor is an essential part of the Christian story, and the tradition of the Upside-Down Kingdom that I finally discovered in my own heritage of the Churches of Christ.

Two of those traditions are rooted in sixteenth-century Europe. One — the one in which I was raised — is rooted in the nineteenth-century American frontier. Yet, in spite of their particularity in time and space — or perhaps I should say, because of that particularity — these three traditions have pointed me, consistently and unmistakably, to the gospel that was proclaimed in the primitive church — the gospel of the good news of God's unmerited grace.

Luther and the Anabaptists: Joined and Divided

Even though I have remained in the Churches of Christ, it is safe to say that Martin Luther and the Anabaptists of the sixteenth century have played the preeminent role in helping me understand the genius of Scripture and thereby defining my theological, moral, and personal development. Over the years, in fact, my sense of vocation has rested more and more on the paradox of justification that I learned from Luther and the paradox of sanctification that I learned from the Anabaptists.

In light of the historic theological tension between these two traditions, many Lutherans and Mennonites today would no doubt wince to hear someone claim spiritual and theological roots in both these traditions. I well remember, in fact, the stares of disbelief that emerged on the faces of many Lutheran scholars when I made that very claim at the "Vocation of a Lutheran College" conference at Carthage College in 1997.

In response, I would make several observations. First, historians often speak of the Anabaptists as if they were the only "radicals" of the Reformation. Yet, I would argue that there were two radicals of the Reformation. One was Luther, who could not have been more radical in the way he framed the paradox of justification. The other was the Anabaptist tradition that could not have been more radical in the way it framed the paradox of sanctification.

Second, I would argue that the paradox of justification and the paradox of sanctification are really two dimensions of a richly over- *xxvii* arching paradox that I would call "the paradox of the gospel." How could it be, for example, that Luther's advice to "sin boldly" and the Anabaptists' advice to "take up one's cross" could be legitimate and complementary expressions of the same Christian tradition? How could Luther's insistence that no one can possibly be good enough to save one's self — how could that affirmation possibly harmonize with the emphasis the Anabaptists placed on a lifestyle of selfless living? Yet, I am convinced that these two radical ways of defining the Christian tradition — two ways that seem at first glance so completely contradictory — are really two sides of the same Christian gospel and, when yoked together, frame the grandest paradox of all.

And third, the tragedy of the Reformation lay in the fact that the themes of radical justification and radical sanctification ripped apart, with Lutherans laying claim to the one and Anabaptists claiming the other.

In the beginning of the Reformation, there was hope that the paradox of the gospel could be kept intact. While Luther clearly built his long-term reform around the doctrine of justification by grace through faith, he also embraced the notion of radical sanctification in his early years, and even argued for the kind of "gathered church" that would be the hallmark of the Anabaptist tradition. But alas, the pressures of maintaining a state church led Luther to scuttle that vision and in time he became one of the most vehement opponents of the Anabaptist movement.[10]

At the same time, while the Anabaptists clearly built their reform on the moral principle of sanctification, they also claimed the doctrine of justification by grace through faith.[11] But when faced with brutal persecution from the magisterial reformers, they turned on Luther and his theology and, in Leonard Verduin's words,

> rubbed in his face the words he had put down in his *Deutsche Messe.* Speaking of their congregation of believers, they twitted their Lutheran antagonists. "Your own prophet Martin Luther," they declared, "has written about such gatherings in a little book entitled *Deutsche Messe,* as follows: 'Men ought to gather in a place apart behind closed doors.' . . . but he added, 'I am not brave enough to make a beginning with that sort of thing, lest it be considered as an act of sedition.'"[12]

10. Leonard Verduin has documented these dynamics in "Luther's Dilemma: Restitution or Reformation?" in Kenneth Strand, ed., *The Dawn of Modern Civilization* (Ann Arbor Publications). Strand reports, for example, that Luther envied the Waldensians and wrote, "By God's grace there is found with you such a fine and disciplined way of life, no such gourmandizing and drinking, no such swearing and cursing, no such ostentation and wickedness, as is found with us." In 1523 he confided to his friend Nicholas Hausmann that "the plan is in future times to admit no one to communion unless he has been heard and has responded satisfactorily in regard to the faith; the rest we shall exclude." In his *Deutsche Messe* of 1526, he still held out hope for such a vision: "Those who desire seriously to be Christians and confess the gospel by word and by deed, these should enter their names in a ledger and meet somewhere in a house by themselves for the purpose of prayer, reading of Scripture, baptism, receiving the Sacrament and performing other Christian liturgical acts. . . ." This was in essence the Anabaptist understanding of the "gathered church." However, Luther also confided, "But I cannot gather such a Church or congregation as yet, for I do not have the people for it." Pp. 175-77.

11. Walter Klaassen offers numerous examples of this emphasis in his *Anabaptism in Outline* (Scottdale, Pa.: Herald Press, 1981), pp. 41-71.

12. Verduin, p. 180.

In time, most Anabaptists all but abandoned Luther's radical understanding of justification by grace through faith and, instead, built their house on the moral principle of sanctification. And as Verduin notes, "The honeymoon between Luther and the Restitutionists was over."[13]

Reflections on the Present Book

What does this brief excursion into the history of the Reformation have to do with this book? Just this: I am neither Lutheran nor Anabaptist in any formal sense. Yet, these two traditions have profoundly shaped my own sense of vocation of which this book is a faithful reflection.

As a result, Luther stands at the center of this book and is finally responsible for such emphases as these:

> We must admit that Christian faith will invariably stand at odds with the life of the mind if we envision that faith in terms of absolutistic principles, sterile legal codes, or moral imperatives that require from us no reflection, no creativity, and no imagination. But dynamic Christian faith — the kind of faith that can sustain the life of the mind — requires that we think about the Christian faith in paradoxical terms.

Or again,

> If I confess the sovereignty of God and the finitude of humankind, I confess as well that my reason is inevitably impaired and that my knowledge is always incomplete. Quite simply, this position means that many of the judgments I make in the context of the academy may well be fragmentary and partial. Indeed, they may be wrong.

13. Verduin, p. 180.

Or again,

> After all, the fact that I am a finite human being means that I
> am a creature of a particular time and a particular place and a
> particular culture. How can I possibly transcend these limita-
> tions? After all, I am not God.

Or again,

> [To confess that I am not God] empowers me to critically
> scrutinize my own theories, my own judgments, and my own
> understandings. Once I make this confession, it becomes very
> difficult to absolutize my judgments and interpretations or to
> elevate my opinions to the status of an orthodoxy to which
> everyone else must conform. No, once I make this confession,
> I must be open to other voices — voices from other cultures,
> other races, other ethnic traditions; voices from different
> places and different historical periods; yes, even voices from
> other religions.

At the same time, Anabaptist leaders like Menno Simons,
Conrad Grebel, and Michael Sattler also stand at the center of this
book and are responsible for such emphases as these:

> But the Christian gospel requires more than openness. It re-
> quires compassion as well, and the kind of compassion the
> gospel invokes is a universal, indiscriminate compassion that
> reaches beyond the clan or the tribe to the stranger.

Or again,

> I submit that when we focus our students' attention on the
> poor, the marginalized, and the oppressed, we accomplish a
> number of objectives that must be fundamental to the mis-

sion of any Christian institution of higher learning. First, we encourage our students to take seriously the ambiguity of the human situation, for nothing can be more ambiguous than human life that is marginalized. Second, by teaching in this way, we allow our students to see the very face of God, for according to Scripture, God wears the face of the poor and has taken upon himself the ambiguity of the human situation. Third, by teaching in this way, we create a marvelous opportunity to encourage our students to serve as agents of peace and justice and reconciliation.

Conclusions

What conclusions, then, might we draw from all of this?

First, if we hope to serve as effective teachers and scholars, then our work must proceed from a profound sense of vocation. That is a fact of life for those who identify themselves as Christian and those who do not.

Second, for those who find their identity in the work of scholarship, on the one hand, and their commitment to the Christian faith, on the other, framing a sense of vocation is no easy task. This is because they inevitably live in the world of paradox — a world defined by particularistic commitments that often stand in contrast with a radical search for truth.

Third, because the Christian scholar lives in a paradoxical world, a meaningful sense of vocation might well draw on a paradoxical vision or a paradoxical way of framing reality.

Fourth, if a Christian scholar hopes to ground her sense of vocation in the Christian faith at all, then she must find resources in the Christian faith itself. The first task in the "theological exploration of vocation" is to ask how our faith traditions can provide us with a meaningful sense of calling. But for those of us who have found that calling in the life of the mind, the next task is to ask how our religious faith can sustain us in the work we have been called to do.

The book we call *The Vocation of the Christian Scholar: How Christian Faith Can Sustain the Life of the Mind* is a text that takes up that challenge. For the burden of this book is to ask, "How can I find in my faith meaningful support for the vocation of thinking, writing, and teaching?" I have found that support in the biblical text, mediated to me through two of the great theological traditions of the Reformation: the theology of Martin Luther and the theology of the sixteenth-century Anabaptists. Others find support in other Christian traditions. And still others find support in religious traditions that are not Christian at all.

The point is simply this: if we who are scholars wish to engage "the theological exploration of vocation" in a meaningful way, then we must bring our religious faith and convictions into constant dialogue with our lives and with our work. To do less might well suggest that we have embraced not a vocation but merely a career.

Acknowledgments

There is a sense in which this book began in 1992 when William Adrian and I applied for a grant from the Lilly Endowment, hoping to pursue a project that would document the "status" of church-related higher education in the United States. The Endowment, however, turned us down flat. They had no interest, they said, in funding a project that would "report" on the "status" of that enterprise. But they would be interested, they said, in funding a project that promised tangible assistance to church-related institutions that seek to live more fruitfully out of their historic Christian missions. Adrian and I then framed a project that we hoped would meet those requirements. That project resulted in the book *Models for Christian Higher Education: Strategies for Success in the Twenty-first Century* (Eerdmans, 1997).

I conceive of this current volume as an extenuation of the desire to offer "tangible assistance." But the assistance offered in this case is not only to *institutions* but especially to *individual faculty* who want to connect Christian faith with scholarship and teaching in meaningful and effective ways. While many of those faculty teach in church-related institutions, many others teach in public or private institutions that claim no connection to the Christian tradition at all.

This book draws in certain respects on the earlier *Models* volume. But it is a very different sort of book. While the *Models* volume highlighted *institutional* narratives, this book highlights theological understandings of the Christian faith. And while the *Models* volume explored ways in which Christian colleges and universities can more effectively appropriate their historic missions, this book explores primarily the ways in which individual faculty can appropriate Christian theology to sustain the life of the mind and to enhance their scholarship and their classroom teaching. Indeed, this book begins with the premise that Christian scholars who hope to connect their scholarship and teaching with their Christian faith in a meaningful way must learn to think theologically and to ground their work in a clear theological vision.

This little book is intended to be provocative, not prescriptive. In other words, it doesn't set out to tell faculty *how* to relate faith to learning. Rather, it seeks to provide some of the theological tools they need in order to accomplish that objective for themselves. Frankly, this book assumes that Christian faculty are creative and imaginative and fully capable of relating faith to learning in meaningful ways, if they possess the theological tools to do so.

Most — though not all — of the chapters in this book originated as oral presentations. The bulk of this preface — that is, the section on vocation — originated as a presentation for a faculty retreat at Goshen College in the fall of 2002. Chapter two is a revised version of the Heugli Lecture on Church-Related Higher Education for 1999, presented at Valparaiso University in March of that year and entitled, "Musing on Tuesday's Questions: Luther in the Context of the American Enlightenment." Chapter four originated as a lecture entitled, "How the Lutheran Heritage Can Sustain the Life of the Mind," a presentation made in 1997 to presidents and provosts of institutions that belong to the Lutheran Educational Conference of North America. The section on Mennonite heritage in chapter four draws extensively from a lecture presented at Goshen College in 1997, "My Vision for Christian Higher Education in the Mennonite Context." Chapter five originated as a presentation at a faculty workshop at Concordia University, Austin, Texas, in 1997. And chapter seven was commissioned by the University Commons at Mercer University for a book entitled, *Gladly Learn and Gladly Teach: Living Out One's Calling in the Twenty-first Century Academy.*

Much of this material has already been published in various renditions in scattered books and journals, and I am grateful to the following for permission to republish here:

PREFACE
New Wineskins magazine (www.wineskins.org)

CHAPTER TWO
The Cresset: A Review of Literature, Arts, and Public Affairs, Valparaiso University

CHAPTER FOUR
From Mission to Marketplace: Papers and Proceedings 1997, Lutheran Educational Conference of North America; *Trying Times: American Catholic Higher Education in the Twentieth Century,* ed. William M. Shea and Alice Gallin (Atlanta: Scholars Press, 1999); *Intersections* (a publication for colleges and universities of the Evangelical Lutheran Church in America), Winter 1998; *The Southern Baptist Educator* (the news journal of the Association of Southern Baptist Colleges and Schools), Fall 1998 and Second Quarter, 1999

Gladly Learn and Gladly Teach: Living Out One's Calling in the Twenty-first Century Academy (Macon: Mercer University Press, 2005)

For the opportunity to undertake this project, I am especially indebted to the Lilly Endowment, whose generous funding made possible the years of thought and reflection that finally bear their fruit in this publication. I also wish to thank the faculties of the following institutions who interacted with me in critical and helpful ways when I shared portions of this material as oral presentations: Abilene Christian University, Baylor University, California Lutheran University, Carson-Newman College, Concordia University (Austin, Texas), Concordia University (River Forest, Illinois), Goshen College, Gustavus Adolphus College, Luther College, Pacific Lutheran University, Pepperdine University, St. Louis University, Texas Lutheran University, Valparaiso University, William Jewell College, and faculty representing a number of Lutheran institutions who critiqued this material at the "Vocation of a Lutheran College" conference that convened at Carthage College in 1997.

xxxv

I am grateful to the following individuals who took the time to read this material and to make a variety of helpful suggestions: William S. Banowsky, Andrew Benton, Paul Boyer, Robert Cochran, David Davenport, John Marson Dunaway, Susan VanZanten Gallagher, James L. Heft, Harold Heie, Samuel S. Hill Jr., Milton Horne, Douglas Jacobsen, Patricia O'Connell Killen, DeAne Lagerquist, George Marsden, Lanney Mayer, Richard Mouw, Mark Schwehn, Chris Soper, Don Thompson, James Turner, Diane Winston, Alan Wolfe, Nicholas Wolterstorff, and Robert Wuthnow. I cannot begin to name the many others who have contributed to my thinking through private conversation or whose books and articles have provided invaluable insights.

Finally, I thank my wife, Jan, who has shared conversation with me regarding these issues for many, many years, and whose insights never fail to stimulate my thinking. She has helped sustain my "life of the mind."

RICHARD T. HUGHES
Malibu, California
March 2004

Introduction

"**C**AN CHRISTIAN FAITH SUSTAIN THE LIFE OF THE MIND?" To many academics, this question would seem absurd. In their judgment, religion is fundamentally dogmatic while the life of the mind requires openness, creativity, and imagination. This stereotypical assumption regarding the nature of religion in general and Christianity in particular has contributed significantly over the past one hundred years to the divorce between faith and learning on countless campuses throughout the United States. For Christian scholars, therefore, it is hard to imagine a more pressing consideration than this: Can Christian faith sustain the life of the mind? This small book will seek to address that question.

In raising this question, I do not mean to suggest that the other great religions of the world lack resources to sustain the life of the mind. Each of them possesses extraordinary resources, and scholars with allegiance to these traditions — Buddhism, Hinduism, Judaism, and Islam, for example — should ask in careful and deliberate ways how their traditions can and do sustain the life of the mind.

This book, however, inquires about Christianity in particular, and it does so on behalf of those many scholars who claim the Christian tradition and who teach in both public and private institutions, and also on behalf of those many colleges and universities who claim a relationship to the Christian faith.

If we have any reasonable hope to find satisfactory answers to our question, we first must inquire, "What do we mean by the phrase, 'the life of the mind'"? Surely this fundamentally human activity has little to do with activities like memorizing lists or manipulating data. Instead, it has everything to do with at least four dimensions of human thought.

First, the life of the mind commits us to a rigorous and disciplined search for truth. This dimension of the life of the mind presupposes something that both the Bible and human experience make very clear, namely, that we are not gods, but finite human beings with very human limitations. This notion has enormous implications for those of us who serve as scholars. It means that our intellectual vision is clouded, our perception limited, and our understanding flawed. If we take seriously this fundamental aspect of human experience, then we have no other choice but to search for truth. To do otherwise is to deny not only the plain teachings of the Christian faith but a most basic reality of human existence.

Second, in the context of the search for truth, the life of the mind entails genuine conversation with a diversity of perspectives and worldviews that are different from our own. In this context, "diversity" is the operative term. Diversity is critical to higher education, for when we take seriously cultures, religions, and perspectives that are different from our own, we learn to see the world through someone else's eyes. More than that, we learn to critique ourselves from another's point of view. If we memorize all the historical data in the world, if we find ourselves on the cutting edge of scientific thought and development, and if we hone our technological skills to perfection — if we do all this, but never learn to critique ourselves from the perspective of another culture or another religious tradition, then all of our claims to be educated people ring hollow indeed.

Third, the life of the mind involves critical thinking as we seek to analyze and assess the worldviews and perspectives we have studied. Critical thinking, analysis, and assessment — these terms presuppose that we have a place to stand, a point of reference from which we can evaluate what we have studied. For the believer, that point of reference is clearly the Christian faith.

But here things get tricky, for it is always tempting to elevate our perception of our reference point to a position of infallible judgment. When this happens, we never really take diversity seriously, never really hear those other voices, never really engage other cultures, other perspectives, and other religious traditions. When this happens, critical thinking evaporates into absolutistic thinking, and the search for truth is dead.

Critical thinking, then, demands a point of reference that can be critiqued even as it seeks to critique, even when that point of reference is our particular understanding of the Christian faith. After all, our particular understanding is just that — our particular understanding. This is why we must employ other perspectives to chasten our fundamental point of reference, even as we judge those other perspectives by our particular point of view. In a nutshell, this means that we must never succumb to patterns of thought that are merely one-dimensional. Instead, we must learn to think dialectically, even paradoxically, as we seek to bring a variety of perspectives into dialogue with one another.

And fourth, the life of the mind involves intellectual creativity. We embrace intellectual creativity when we seek to make connections between a variety of categories, when we think new thoughts, when we develop new insights, and when we create new and fresh ways of understanding old material. In a word, intellectual creativity requires imagination.

But there can be neither creativity nor imagination apart from the other categories we have just discussed. Creative imagination can thrive only when we engage in a rigorous pursuit of truth, since apart from that pursuit our minds stagnate. Again, creative imagination can thrive only when we allow a diversity of conversation partners to challenge our thinking, since without those partners, we risk intellectual paralysis. And finally, creative imagination can thrive only when we embrace dialectical, even paradoxical ways of thinking, since a collision of opposing perspectives can generate the energy upon which the imagination feeds.

The pressing questions that we must raise and seek to answer, then, are these: Can Christian faith equip us to pursue the truth wherever that pursuit may lead? Can Christian faith empower the believing scholar to engage a wide range of conversation partners, even when those partners hold positions that may threaten our most cherished beliefs? And finally, does Christian faith empower the Christian scholar to think in paradoxical terms, to simultaneously hold to conflicting positions, and to allow that conflict to generate imaginative creativity?

From the outset, we must admit that Christian faith will invariably stand at odds with the life of the mind if we envision that faith in terms of absolutistic principles, sterile legal codes, or moral imperatives that require from us no reflection, no creativity, and no imagination. But dynamic Christian faith — the kind of faith that can sustain the life of the mind — requires that we think about the Christian faith in paradoxical terms, and that we explore the *meaning* of Christian themes in *relation* to the world in which we live. We must ask, for example, about the *meaning* of God's sovereignty in relation to politics and education, about the *meaning* of God's love in relation to human relationships, about the *meaning* of God's wrath in relation to peace and justice, about the *meaning* of creation in relation to the environment, about the *meaning* of the cross in relation to materialism and poverty, and on and on we could go.

In a word, dynamic Christian faith requires that we learn to make *connections* and to think creatively about the *meaning* of what we believe. We call this kind of thinking, "theology," and if we have any hope that Christian faith might sustain the life of the mind, every Christian scholar must learn to work as a theologian in his or her own right.

Theological work, however, is not the same as Bible study. One can study the Bible simply to learn biblical facts and never embrace theological work at all. We do theology only when we begin to reflect creatively on the meaning of the biblical text. And it is only when we ask in creative and imaginative ways about the relation of the biblical message to the world in which we live — it is only then that Christian faith can sustain the life of the mind.

In order to reflect creatively on the meaning of the biblical text, however, we must first be clear on what kind of book the Bible really is. If we conceive of the Bible as nothing more than a rulebook, or a scientific manual, or a legal code, or a divinely-authored constitution whose contents we can master with ease, then there is very little room for creative reflection on the meaning of the biblical text. In fact, there is very little room for interpretive work at all. Rather, the Bible simply means what it says and says what it means with clarity and scientific precision. If we view the Bible in these terms, then we can only view as perverse those who disagree with our particular reading of the biblical text.

This view of the Bible offers precious little support for the life of the mind. There can be no disciplined search for truth, for truth has already been defined. There can be no serious conversation with people who represent a diversity of cultural and religious perspectives, since we know in advance that people who hold perspectives different from our own have nothing to contribute to the conversation in any event. Critical thinking that discriminates between competing worldviews and perspectives is finally pointless since we have rejected competing worldviews and perspectives from the outset. And creativity falls by the wayside as well, since creativity is nurtured by imaginative inquiry, not by codified legal constraints.

But the Bible is not a rulebook, a scientific manual, a legal code, or a divinely-authored constitution. Rather, the Bible is a *theological* text, that is, a book about God. Accordingly, the Bible invites each of us to reflect on the meaning of that which transcends our understanding: the infinite Lord of the universe. Precisely because the subject of the Bible — the living God — transcends our poor ability to understand, it calls on each of us to respond with wonder, creative imagination, and rational inquiry.

Two points flow from this conception of the biblical text. First, if the Bible is, indeed, the sort of text we have described, then it must be obvious that the Bible requires interpretation and that no one can legitimately claim a corner on the market of God's truth. And second, if the Bible is a *theological* text — a book about God — it calls on every Christian to serve as a theologian, that is, one who thinks about the *meaning* of God and the *meaning* of the Christian faith.

Unfortunately, however, many Christian scholars have never learned to think theologically about the meaning of the Christian faith. Though highly educated in narrow specialties, many Christian scholars essentially remain at a Sunday school level of theological literacy. This is why Christianity and the life of the mind so often stand at odds, even at many Christian institutions of higher learning. And this is why so many Christian scholars, even those who *want* to integrate Christian faith and scholarship in meaningful and productive ways, find it difficult to do so. The truth is, the successful integration of faith and learning demands a certain level of theological literacy and expertise. Otherwise, all our attempts to relate faith to learning will inevitably prove abortive.

This small book, then, will seek to ask how Christian faith can sustain the life of the mind, but it will do so in a variety of ways. In chapter two, we will ask how the "religion of the Republic" defines the values of the modern academy in the United States. In chapter three, we will ask, in rather broad terms, about the meaning of the Christian faith and how the Christian tradition might interact with the values of the academy in meaningful ways. In chapter four, we will ask about four different Christian traditions and how those traditions can sustain the life of the mind. These include the Roman Catholic tradition, but also the three great Reformation traditions of the sixteenth century: Reformed, Anabaptist, and Lutheran.

In chapter five, I use my own classroom teaching as an illustration of how a commitment to some of the great themes of Christian theology can undergird both the form and content of our teaching. As far as I am concerned, everything about my teaching finally rests on explicitly Christian supports. Precisely because I am a Christian scholar, I seek to maintain an open classroom in which my students can raise any questions they wish. Precisely because I am a Christian scholar, I seek to nurture in my students a hunger and thirst for truth. Precisely because I am a Christian scholar, I encourage my students to critically assess not only the perspectives of others, but their own perspectives as well. And precisely because I am a Christian scholar, I encourage my students to approach their studies with imagination and creativity. The fact is, those who name the name of Christ can grow into first-class scholars and teachers, not *in spite of* our Christian commitments, but *because of* those commitments.

In chapter six, we inquire into those nagging and troublesome questions of distinctiveness and proclamation. In other words, how distinctive must a Christian scholar's work finally turn out to be, and when and how might a Christian scholar use the classroom as a vehicle for the proclamation of the Christian gospel?

In chapter seven, we return quite explicitly to the theme of vocation and ask about the vocation of the Christian college. The question that drives this chapter is, "What makes church-related education Christian?"

In the postscript, we explore the relation of the tragic dimensions of human life to the question that frames the substance of this book: how Christian faith can sustain the life of the mind. But here again, this question emerges in the context of personal narrative, journey, and vocation.

Before we move to chapter two, one final word is in order. Christian academicians often ask in what ways their teaching and scholarship might differ from teaching and scholarship carried out in the mainstream academy. In other words, what makes one a Christian scholar? These are questions that anticipate our discussion in chapter six, but they are such fundamental questions that we must briefly consider them now.

Professor Paul Griffiths of the University of Chicago once remarked that "one is a Christian scholar if one understands one's work to be based upon and framed by and always in the service of one's identity as a Christian."[1] If we take these words seriously, then we are forced to admit that the most important consideration in Christian scholarship is one of motivation. The question then becomes, "*Why* do we do what we do?" Even if I teach a class in which my commitment to the Christian faith is not immediately apparent, I still serve as a Christian scholar if I understand my work "to be based upon and framed by and always in the service of [my] identity as a Christian."

Yet, while the question of motivation may be the most fundamental issue at stake, it is not the last word, for scholars who are driven by Christian faith to engage in the life of the mind will find a variety of ways in which their Christian commitments will play themselves out. How that works may depend on one's discipline, the nature of one's educational institution, one's own presuppositions and those of one's students, and a host of other factors. Yet, I am convinced that in every conceivable instance, a scholar's Christian faith can express itself in the highest and finest kind of scholarship — a scholarship committed to search for truth, to engage a variety of conversation partners, to critique all perspectives, even one's own, and to nurture creative imagination.

1. Professor Paul Griffiths, University of Chicago Divinity School, in a question-and-answer session following his lecture, "Seeking Egyptian Gold," at Lilly Fellows Program meeting, Valparaiso University, October 8, 1999.

CHAPTER TWO

The Religion of the Republic
and the Life of the Mind

SOME TIME AGO, I SPOKE TO THE FACULTY AND ADMINISTRA-
tion of a midwestern Lutheran college on the power of the Lutheran tradition to sustain the life of the mind. Because I am convinced that Lutherans possess theological resources that are
uniquely situated for this task, I urged those in my audience to do all
they could to enhance the Lutheran character of the school.

Later, I received a letter from a retired member of that faculty,
writing to express his skepticism that what I had commended
could ever be achieved. It was clear that he took no joy in this report. He wrote that while many of the older professors cared
deeply about the Lutheran character of the institution, these people were in the process of retiring. Typically, he said, their younger
replacements were not committed to the Lutheran character of
the college, but rather "to excellence in their disciplines and, in
many cases, to the goal of greater diversity in the college community." Accordingly, he wrote, many of the younger teachers "would
find a discussion of the issues you raise[d in your presentation
here] to be uninteresting and irrelevant to [our modern] world."
In fact, he concluded, some will view the college as fundamentally
"tribal . . . until most vestiges of Lutheran connections are eliminated."

My correspondent described in almost classic terms the dilemma that faces countless church-related colleges and universities.

We might state that dilemma in the form of a question: How can those of us who work in the field of Christian higher education nurture diversity, openness, and academic freedom, on the one hand, and at the very same time ground our work in the presuppositions of the Christian faith?

If some professors and some institutions resolve this dilemma in favor of diversity and academic integrity and, in the process, slight the Christian faith, faculty members who teach in more conservative church-related schools often work in the opposite direction. Typically, if they have to choose — and they often feel that they must — these people are far more concerned to nurture the Christian character of their institutions than to nurture traditional academic values. Not surprisingly, these institutions seldom compete at the highest academic levels, but they are often successful at sustaining religious commitment.

The problem we face is obvious: How can Christian institutions of higher learning honor the integrity of the Christian faith and the integrity of the academic enterprise at the same time? And to make that question even more pointed, is it possible for these two sides of the equation to sustain and reinforce one another?

Living in Two Worlds Simultaneously

To begin our inquiry, we first must ask about the nature of this academic world in which so many of us live and move and have our being. In response to that question, we must acknowledge that American higher education is in many ways a child of the American Enlightenment. In making this assertion, I do not mean to suggest that the Enlightenment is the only intellectual tradition that has shaped American higher education. But I do mean to suggest that for almost two hundred years, American higher education has embraced a set of values that were fundamental to the Enlightenment in the United States. Preeminent among those values was a commitment to search for truth through free and open discussion. Thomas Jefferson put it well when he wrote

> that truth is great and will prevail if left to herself, that she is the proper and sufficient antagonist to error, and has nothing to fear from the conflict, unless by human interposition disarmed of her natural weapons, free argument and debate. . . .[1]

This commitment stands so completely at the core of higher education in the United States that when we hear of institutions that curtail the right of free and open discussion, most of us conclude that those institutions can hardly be regarded as serious players in the academic arena.

But there is a second reason for beginning our exploration with a consideration of the American Enlightenment. In spite of the pivotal role the Enlightenment has played in American higher education, a growing number of Christian scholars have embraced in recent years the position that the Enlightenment is the root of secularization and the enemy of Christian faith. Many of these scholars have therefore embraced the postmodern world with great enthusiasm. In their judgment, the postmodern vision will grant them a seat at the academic banquet table that the Enlightenment has for so long denied them.

If one takes this position, however, one builds around oneself an artificial box and imposes upon oneself a variety of constraints that are simply needless.

In the first place, the Enlightenment expressed itself in a variety of ways. When Christian scholars rail against the Enlightenment, I suspect that most have in mind the extremes of Enlightenment thought that translated into naturalism and radical empiricism. It is

1. Thomas Jefferson, "Bill for Establishing Religious Freedom," in Julian P. Boyd, ed., *The Papers of Thomas Jefferson*, vol. 2 (Princeton: Princeton University Press, 1950), p. 549.

true that some Enlightenment thinkers embraced an empirical bias that left little room for faith, for the unseen, or for religious considerations of any kind. But other Enlightenment thinkers grounded their moral vision squarely in a religious framework. As serious Christian scholars, therefore, we must be careful not to reject the Enlightenment out of hand and throw the proverbial baby out with the bath water.

When we turn our attention to the postmodern world, we must recognize that, just as there are many versions of Enlightenment thought, so there are many versions of postmodern theory. Some Christian scholars apparently find attractive the relativistic dimensions that characterize *some* postmodern thinking. When postmodern theorists argue that no single ideology is finally any more compelling than any other, some Christian scholars contend that, in the interest of consistency, Christianity deserves a place at the academic banquet table alongside all the other guests. But this strikes me as a highly questionable strategy since, in effect, it courts a vision that relativizes Christian faith, just as it relativizes every other ideology.

At the same time, to the extent that postmodernism affirms that human beings cannot escape their own subjectivity, postmodernism stands shoulder to shoulder with the best insights of the Christian faith. Christian theology has always claimed that God alone is God and that all human beings are finite, that is, caught in a web of their own limitations. At this point, Christian faith and postmodernism can surely work hand in glove.

I am suggesting, then, that we will make a grave mistake if we view the Enlightenment and postmodern theory as mutually exclusive in every conceivable instance. Instead, if we seek to be serious Christian scholars, we will stand in the gap between these two ways of viewing the world. We must realize that each of these perspectives can contribute much to the task of higher education *per se*, and much to the enterprise of Christian scholarship in particular. Indeed, readers of these pages will quickly discover that I myself often emerge as an Enlightenment rationalist, but — in the very next chapter, perhaps — as a postmodern visionary. If this seems like a paradox, it is a paradox I embrace with considerable enthusiasm.

The Work of Sidney E. Mead

Because the Enlightenment has been so badly maligned in recent years, I want to begin by examining a side of the American Enlightenment that I find potentially friendly to scholarship broadly conceived and to Christian scholarship in particular. We will make this journey by exploring the work of Sidney E. Mead.

Widely known in the 1960s and 1970s as the dean of historians of American religion, Mead spent a lifetime exploring the religious dimensions of the American Enlightenment. In one of his books, *The Nation with the Soul of a Church,* he developed an extended argument for how religion sustained — and continues to sustain — the democratic institutions of the United States. Mead's argument holds great implications for those of us who work in the field of higher education. After all, to ask how religious faith might sustain the democratic traditions of the nation is not radically different from asking how religious faith might sustain the life of the mind in the context of American higher education. I trust the relationship between these two questions will become more obvious as we move along.

Mead argued that American democracy rests upon a theological foundation that he often described as the religion of the Republic or, alternately, the theology of the Republic. We can best understand this religious vision if we pay close attention to the Declaration of Independence. Most Americans recognize the Declaration as a political document, but the Declaration was and is a theological document as well. Indeed, Thomas Jefferson rooted the Declaration squarely in classical Deism.

What was Deism, and who were the Deists? The Deists of the seventeenth and eighteenth centuries had searched for a way to terminate the religious wars that plagued Europe in the aftermath of the sixteenth-century Reformation. The Bible, they argued, was in many ways the cause of these conflicts because the Bible was both complex and susceptible to a host of interpretations. But God had authored, they claimed, a second book, a book they called the Book of Nature. If the Bible was complex, this second book was simple. And if the Bible was susceptible to a host of conflicting interpretations, this second book taught clearly and unambiguously the essential doctrines of every major religious tradition. Chief among those doctrines were the twin affirmations that God exists and that his existence guarantees the moral structure of the universe.

We must come to see that the political affirmations of the Declaration rest squarely on these two cardinal principles of the Deist creed. The Declaration, in fact, never invoked the God of the Bible or the God of traditional Judaism or Christianity. We find here no appeals to "the God of Abraham, Isaac, and Jacob" or to "our Lord and Savior Jesus Christ." Instead, the Declaration appeals clearly and deliberately to "Nature and Nature's God," that is, the God that all human beings can know in God's second book, the Book of Nature. Likewise, the Declaration proclaims that the universe embodies a fundamental moral structure. Jefferson described that moral structure with these words:

> We hold these truths to be self-evident, that all men are created equal, that they are endowed by their Creator with certain unalienable rights, that among these are Life, Liberty, and the pursuit of Happiness.

When we understand the theological dimensions of the Declaration of Independence, we begin to understand what Mead had in mind when he spoke of the theology of the Republic. In Mead's judgment, this theology legitimated the right of every human being to search for truth and to frame the truth as he or she saw fit. According to Mead, the theology of the Republic legitimated as well the First Amendment to the Constitution of the United States: "Congress shall make no law respecting an establishment of religion, or prohibiting the free exercise thereof." And "the most constant strand" in this theology of the Republic, Mead believed, was "the primacy of God over all human institutions."

To this point, we have explored only half of Mead's theology of the Republic. If Mead began by affirming "the primacy of God over all human institutions," he stated time and again the corollary to that proposition, namely, the fact that "no man is God." That affirmation, Mead wrote in an especially poignant passage,

> is what I understand to be the functional meaning of "God" in human experience. Whatever "God" may be, if indeed being is applicable to "God," a concept of the infinite seems to me necessary if we are to state the all-important fact about man: that he is finite. This is the premise of all democratic institutions. It is the essential dogma of the religion of the Republic.[2]

Two themes, then, stand at the center of Mead's understanding of the religion of the Republic: the finitude of humankind and the primacy of God over all human institutions. According to Mead, this profoundly theological vision has made possible the democratic experience that Americans have enjoyed now for well over two hundred years.

At this point, two caveats are in order. First, we must acknowledge that the Deist tradition that helped sustain the democratic institutions of the United States was not orthodox Christianity, mainly because it denied the divinity of Jesus Christ. But we should not for that reason dismiss this vision as secularism, humanism, or atheism, as many Christians over the years have been prone to do. We are dealing here with a profoundly religious faith, that is, a faith in an

2. Sidney E. Mead, *The Nation with the Soul of a Church* (New York: Harper and Row, 1975), pp. 9-10. See also p. 119.

infinite power that the eighteenth-century proponents of this vision referred to as "God." Second, while this civic faith of the Republic is in many ways the foundation for all higher education in the United States, Christian higher education included, we must come to see that Christian higher education rests on a second foundation as well — the great theological principles of the Christian religion. We must therefore ask how these two religious traditions can interact with one another in fruitful and productive ways. That must be our fundamental question if we have any hope of resolving the dilemma with which we began, that is, if we have any hope of nurturing simultaneously the life of the mind, on the one hand, and particularistic Christian faith, on the other.

The Religion of the Republic
and the American Churches

In spite of its profoundly theological core, and in spite of its appeal to the sovereignty of God over all human life, Christians — as Mead points out — have often assailed the religious foundation on which the American experience was built as little more than rank infidelity. Why would this be true?

The reason is not hard to find. The Founders embraced the religion of the Republic as a *universal vision* that would legitimate diversity in the Republic. Put another way, here was a *universal vision* to which all people could relate, regardless of their particular religious persuasions. Indeed, Mead argues that the religion of the Republic is "not only *not* particularistic; it is designedly antiparticularistic."[3]

On the other hand, many Protestants in those early years of the Republic longed for a nation that would be grounded in *particularistic* Christian faith. In other words, they wished for a particularistically Christian America. The First Amendment to the Constitu-

3. Mead, *The Nation with the Soul of a Church*, p. 22.

tion, however, made it impossible for Christians or anyone else to impose particularistic faith on the Republic, either by law or by other means of coercion.

But there still remained the possibility of persuasion. And so, Protestants throughout the nation launched in the early years of the nineteenth century a great revival that we know today as the Second Great Awakening. Indeed, one might well interpret that revival as, at least in part, a massive attempt to Christianize, even Protestantize, the Republic by persuasion, since it would now be impossible to do so by force of law.

In addition, many of those Protestants who sought to Christian-ize the Republic by persuasion sought at the very same time to dis-credit the cosmopolitan theology of the Republic that made possible a pluralistic nation. As far as they were concerned, the Founders who had framed this theology were "infidels," and the theology they ar-ticulated, because it lacked explicit Christian content, was nothing short of "infidelity."[4]

Several examples will suffice. Reverend John M. Mason discov-ered in 1800 that Jefferson's *Notes on Virginia* contained the assertion that "the legitimate powers of government extend to such acts only as are injurious to others. But it does me no injury for my neighbor to say there are twenty Gods, or no God. It neither picks my pocket nor breaks my leg." To Mason, Jefferson had preached both "atheism" and "the morality of devils." Another preacher, the Reverend Clement Clarke Moore, objected to the same Jeffersonian text. Upon reading the *Notes on Virginia,* he found himself "surprised that a book which contains so much infidelity, conveyed in so insidious a manner, should have been extensively circulated in a Christian country, for nearly twenty years, without ever having received a formal answer."[5]

4. On this development, see Mead, *The Nation with the Soul of a Church,* pp. 122-23; and Mead, *The Lively Experiment* (New York: Harper and Row, 1963), pp. 38-54.

5. John M. Mason, *The Voice of Warning to Christians, on the Ensuing Election of a President of the United States* (New York, 1800), p. 20; and Clement Clarke Moore, *Observations upon certain passages in Mr. Jefferson's Notes on Virginia, which appear*

Perhaps the most significant Christian leader to respond to the religion of the Enlightenment was Timothy Dwight, grandson of Jonathan Edwards, president of Yale College from 1795 to 1817, and one of the chief architects of the Second Great Awakening. For Dwight, as for so many other Christians of that age, "infidelity" was a synonym for the religion of the Enlightenment. Accordingly, "infidelity" was a plan "for exterminating Christianity" and offered "no efficacious means of restraining Vice, or promoting Virtue, but, on the contrary encourages Vice and discourages Virtue." In fact, "so evident is the want of morals on the part of Infidels . . . that to say 'A man is an Infidel' is understood . . . as a declaration that he is a plainly immoral man."[6]

This attack which Christian revivalists marshaled against the religion of the Enlightenment bore long-term effects that are still with us, and it is precisely here that Mead's analysis can be helpful to those of us who work in the field of Christian higher education. Indeed, Mead observes that the evangelical attack on the Founders drove a permanent wedge between the particularistic theologies of the churches, on the one hand, and the religion of the Republic, on the other. But it did much more than that. It also drove a wedge between the churches and the centers of higher learning. For if the churches have sought to maintain their particularistic theologies, colleges and universities have sought to maintain a context in which a wide variety of perspectives could thrive. For this reason, Mead writes, "the[se] two parts of the culture simply went their separate ways. . . . The intellectual and religious lives have . . . been separately institutionalized in the universities and denominations respectively. Universities define the intellectual life; denominations define the religious life."[7]

to have a tendency to Subvert Religion, and establish a False Philosophy (New York, 1804), p. 5; both cited in G. Adolf Kock, *Religion of the American Enlightenment* (New York: Thomas Y. Crowell Co., 1968; orig. pub. 1933), pp. 271-72.

6. Cited in Mead, *The Nation with the Soul of a Church*, p. 70.

7. Mead, *The Nation with the Soul of a Church*, p. 124.

But there is more to the story than even this, for the nineteenth-century contest between evangelical Christians and the Founders foreshadowed in certain important respects a very similar struggle that would play itself out in church-related colleges in the United States for over two hundred years. After all, the contest between evangelical Christians and the Founders was a struggle between particularity and universality or, put another way, a struggle between particularity and the affirmation of diversity.

Yet, we should note that while the religion of the Republic promised diversity, those who embraced its tenets often fell short of its lofty ideals. For example, even though Thomas Jefferson penned the words, "We hold these truths to be self-evident, that all men are created equal," he died with numerous slaves still in bondage at Monticello. Or again, Ben Franklin complained of the growing ethnic diversity in Pennsylvania. "This will in a few years become a German Colony," Franklin fretted.

> Instead of Learning our Language, we must learn theirs, or live as in a foreign country. Already the English begin to quit particular Neighborhoods surrounded by Dutch, being uneasy by the Disagreeableness of Dissonant Manners; and in Time, Numbers will probably quit the Province for the same Reason.[8]

If Christians sometimes failed to live out the meaning of the Christian vision, therefore, the Deist Founders sometimes failed to live out the meaning of their vision as well. But these developments should not obscure the fact that in the late eighteenth and early nineteenth centuries, the Deistic Founders of the Republic sought to create a nation where every citizen would be free to embrace or reject any religious sentiment whatsoever. At the same time, many

8. Cited in Robert N. Bellah, *The Broken Covenant: American Civil Religion in Time of Trial* (Chicago: University of Chicago Press, 1992), p. 90.

Christians sought through the Second Great Awakening to create an explicitly Protestant nation. This contest between religious diversity and religious particularity is the very same contest that for two hundred years has posed such a challenge to church-related higher education in the United States.

CHAPTER THREE

Christian Faith and the Life of the Mind

WE NOW MUST ASK, DOES MEAD PROVIDE ANY SOLUTION TO the problem he identifies? How is it possible, in other words, for Christians in the United States to resolve the tension that has always plagued the relationship between particularistic Christianity and the religion of the Republic? And by extension, how is it possible for Christian scholars to resolve the tension created by our simultaneous commitment to diversity, on the one hand, and to a highly particularistic Christian vision, on the other?

Mead does, indeed, offer a solution to this problem. Quite simply, he urges Christians to break through the particularity of their own traditions. Since Mead borrows this concept from the theologian Paul Tillich, we need to hear the way Tillich frames this issue. After exploring the relationship between Christianity and the world religions, Tillich concludes like this:

> Religion cannot come to an end, and a particular religion will be lasting to the degree in which it negates itself as a religion. Thus Christianity will be a bearer of the religious answer as long as it breaks through its own particularity. In the depth of every living religion there is a point at which the religion itself loses its importance, and that to which it points breaks through its particularity, elevating it to spiritual freedom and with it to a vision of the spiritual presence

in other expressions of the ultimate meaning of man's existence.[1]

Reflecting on this passage, Mead writes, "without claiming to understand exactly what Tillich meant by those words, I have my opinion of what 'that' is to which 'every living religion points,' namely, that no man is God."[2] In other words, that to which all religions ultimately point is finally the infinite God, on the one hand, and the finitude of human beings, on the other.

As far as Mead is concerned, this is precisely the vision that animates the theology of the Republic. Thus, he writes,

> When Franklin spoke of "the essentials of every religion" he added that these were "to be found in all the religions we had in our country" though in each "mix'd with other articles" peculiar to that sect. This is not to create a syncretistic common core, but to plumb for the universal which is dressed and disguised in the particularities of doctrine and practice that distinguish one sect from another. This conception enabled them to distinguish between the substance of religion, and its forms exemplified in sectarian tenets and observances.[3]

Accordingly, Mead concludes that "Tillich's view seems . . . implicit in the whole American experience with religious pluralism."[4]

And yet, we know that Americans have sometimes absolutized even the religion of the Republic, insisting that other peoples in other nations must embrace American values precisely as Americans do. When this happens, we find the ingredients for oppression and

1. Paul Tillich, *Christianity and the Encounter of the World Religions* (New York: Columbia University Press, 1963), pp. 96-97.

2. Sidney E. Mead, *The Nation with the Soul of a Church* (New York: Harper and Row, 1975), pp. 9-10.

3. Mead, *The Nation with the Soul of a Church*, p. 60.

4. Mead, *The Nation with the Soul of a Church*, p. 63.

American imperialism. American citizens must therefore break through the particularities of American culture and tradition, just as Christians must break through the particularities of their various cultures and traditions.

What Might It Mean for Christians to "Break Through the Particularities" of Their Own Religious Traditions?

Over the years I have given considerable thought to the question of what it might mean for *Christians* to "break through the particularities" of their own religious traditions. After struggling with this concept for a very long time, I have finally concluded that it holds some very positive implications for the practice of Christian higher education.

At the same time, I have found that this concept is easily misunderstood. Many Christian scholars who hear this notion for the first time quickly conclude that it means the destruction of particularities. Nothing, in my judgment, could be further from the truth. But the notion that we should "break through the particularities" of our faith does involve a paradox. The paradox lies in the fact that when we affirm a particularity, we break through it at the very same time, only to affirm it again and break through it again, and on and on we go, simultaneously affirming and breaking through, affirming and breaking through, affirming and breaking through.

I would argue, in fact, that if we seek to be faithful Christians we have no choice but to embrace the paradox of simultaneously affirming and breaking through the particularities of our faith. This is true for at least five reasons.

The Nature of God

First, the object of our faith must always be God — the Infinite One, the Ultimate One, the Alpha, the Omega, the Creator of all, and the sovereign Lord of the universe. Yet, even though this God must always be the object of my faith, my very finite humanness finally means that I have no ability to conceptualize or describe this infinite God. The best I can do is to operate with symbols that *point to* the Reality that is God. These symbols comprise the particularities of my faith. But even though these symbols are the only means at my disposal that give me the power to speak of God at all, they are grossly inadequate. Their inadequacy arises from the fact that I am finite, my thoughts are finite, and my words are finite. But I seek with these very finite thoughts and words to speak of an infinite God.

By now, it must be obvious why I claim that if we seek to be faithful Christians, we have no choice but to embrace the paradox of affirming and breaking through the particularities of our faith. To break through the particularities of our faith means that we allow those particularities to point us to the infinite God. Conversely, it means that we refuse to view those particularities as ends in themselves, and we refuse to erect those particularities as brittle, dogmatic standards that never point beyond themselves to the God who should be the singular object of our faith. The frightening truth of the matter is simply this: if we refuse to break through those particularities but absolutize them instead, then we have engaged in a reprehensible act of idolatry.

Let me give just one example. In the sixteenth century, Martin Luther embraced the formula, "justification by grace through faith." This notion was for Luther a powerful and dynamic idea, but its power lay in the fact that it pointed beyond itself to the reality of God who offered his grace to sinful human beings. Later in the sixteenth century, however, other Lutheran theologians whom we now call the Scholastic theologians radically transformed Luther's original idea. They still used the words, "justification by grace through faith," but in their hands, that phrase became a litmus test for orthodox Lutheran belief. In other words, it became an end in itself, not a symbol that pointed beyond itself to the one and only Source of "justification by grace through faith."

The Nature of the Bible

The second reason why we must embrace the paradox of simultaneously affirming and breaking through the particularities of our faith lies in the nature of the Bible. In Chapter One, we argued that the Bible is not a rule book, or a scientific manual, or a legal code, or a divinely authored constitution. Instead, we claimed, the Bible is a theological text, that is, a book about God.

But what does that mean for how we might handle the particularities of our faith? If we envision the Bible as a theological text, that is, as a book about God, then the Bible is not a book whose contents we can master. Instead, the Bible points us to a God who masters each of us. According to this conception, the Bible points us not to itself, but rather to the infinite God whose understanding no human being can fathom and who stands in judgment on all our claims that somehow we have captured ultimate truth. This conception of the Bible leaves no place for human pride, but forces each of us to humble ourselves before the throne of God and to acknowledge with Job,

> Surely I spoke of things I did not understand,
> > things too wonderful for me to know.
> My ears had heard of you
> > but now my eyes have seen you.
> Therefore I despise myself
> > And repent in dust and ashes.   (Job 42:3, 5-6)

Or again, if we allow the Bible to point beyond itself to the infinite God, we finally have no choice but to confess with Isaiah, "Woe to me! I am ruined! For I am a man of unclean lips, and I live among a people of unclean lips, and my eyes have seen the King, the LORD Almighty" (Isaiah 6:5).

Can the Bible, viewed in these terms, sustain the life of the mind? It can, indeed, for if the Bible points beyond itself to the infinite God, we have no choice but to search for truth. After all, when we view ourselves in relation to God, we understand how abysmally ignorant we really are. And if the Bible points beyond itself to an infinite God, we have no choice but to engage in serious conversation with a variety of conversation partners, for we know that all perspectives may well shed light on God's eternal truth. And if the Bible points beyond itself to an infinite God, we have no choice but to engage in critical thinking, for we must now discriminate between competing worldviews and perspectives as we seek to understand more fully the nature, the glory, and the will of our Creator. And finally, if the Bible points beyond itself to an infinite God, then we must reach toward that God through expressions of creative imagination.

The Meaning of the Christian Gospel

But there is a third reason why, as faithful Christians, we must break through the particularities of our faith, and it is this: from first to last, the *gospel* is the core of Christian faith, and we must never allow anything to displace it. This is the point the Apostle Paul seeks to make when he argues in 1 Corinthians 15:1-4 that it is the gospel — and only the gospel — that is of first importance. And the gospel, of course, is nothing less than the good news that "God was reconciling the world to himself in Christ" (2 Corinthians 5:19). This is the essence of Christian belief. For that reason, Paul writes,

> Now brothers, I want to remind you of the gospel I preached
> to you, which you received and on which you have taken your
> stand. By this gospel you are saved, if you hold firmly to the

word I preached to you. Otherwise, you have believed in vain. For what I received I passed on to you as of first importance: that Christ died for our sins according to the Scriptures, that he was buried, that he was raised on the third day according to the Scriptures.

Christians must never substitute anything for the gospel — not the Bible, not the sacraments, not our creeds or confessions of faith, not our forms of worship or patterns of church organization, and not our denominational traditions, regardless of the loyalty they may inspire. Rather, though we may affirm all these things, we must at the very same time break through them to the gospel message which is the standard of all Christian faith.

The Neighbor in the Christian Vision

But there is a fourth reason why the Christian gospel demands that we break through the particularities of our faith, for the Christian gospel always points in two directions simultaneously: vertically to God and horizontally to the neighbor. In fact, we could summarize the gospel by saying that just as God extends his grace to us, so we must reflect that grace to the neighbor. But how often have we been guilty of transforming the Christian faith into a set of orthodox propositions that simply stand there in all their splendor and do nothing to connect us either to God or to the neighbor?

In this connection the Old Testament prophet Amos quickly comes to mind. The people Amos addressed carried out their worship with scrupulous attention to the law, but seldom allowed their worship to point beyond itself to the needs of the neighbor. Accordingly, Amos has God cry out,

I hate, I despise your religious feasts;
 I cannot stand your assemblies. . . .

Away with the noise of your songs!
    I will not listen to the music of your harps.
But let justice roll on like a river,
    Righteousness like a never-failing stream!

(Amos 5:21, 23-24)

We think as well of the Pharisees who scrupulously performed the duties of the law, but seldom understood that the real purpose of the law was service to the neighbor. No wonder that Jesus assailed them with these words:

Woe to you, teachers of the law and Pharisees, you hypocrites! You give a tenth of your spices — mint, dill and cummin. But you have neglected the more important matters of the law — justice, mercy and faithfulness. (Matthew 23:23)

Then Jesus concluded, "You should have practiced the latter, without neglecting the former." In other words, there is nothing wrong with orthodox beliefs. But those beliefs must never become ends in themselves. We must affirm them so long as they are biblical and true, but we must at the very same time break through them to those realities to which every Christian doctrine finally points, namely, to God and to the neighbor.

On Surrendering Our Egos

But there is a fifth and final reason why Christians must learn to break through the particularities of their faith, and it is this: the gospel requires that we surrender the single dimension of ourselves that each of us holds most precious, namely, our egos. In other words, the gospel demands that we admit that we are not self-sufficient, that in spite of our pretense to the contrary, we are finally nothing more than finite human beings — broken, alienated, fragmented, and estranged. In a word, the gospel demands that we bow before the sovereignty of God and confess that we are only human beings who cannot possibly save ourselves from the ambiguity of the human situation.

Implications for the Life of the Mind

All five of these ideas ultimately point to one common reality: God alone is God, and we are but human beings who cannot possibly save ourselves. The gospel is simply the good news that God has bridged this gap on our behalf. This is why God must remain the singular object of our faith, why the Bible must always point beyond itself to the God who creates and redeems, and why gratitude for this great gift compels me to care for the neighbor, just as God has cared for me.

The implications of these ideas for the life of the mind are enormous. If I confess the sovereignty of God and the finitude of humankind, I confess as well that my reason is inevitably impaired and that my knowledge is always incomplete. Quite simply, this position means that many of the judgments I make in the context of the academy may well be fragmentary and partial. Indeed, they may be wrong.

After all, the fact that I am a finite human being means that I am a creature of a particular time and a particular place and a particular culture. How can I possibly transcend these limitations? After all, I am not God.

This confession empowers me to critically scrutinize my own theories, my own judgments, and my own understandings. Once I make this confession, it becomes very difficult to absolutize my judgments and interpretations or to elevate my opinions to the status of an orthodoxy to which everyone else must conform. No, once I make this confession, I must be open to other voices — voices from other cultures, other races, other ethnic traditions; voices from different places and different historical periods; yes, even voices from other religions.

But the Christian gospel requires more than openness. It requires compassion as well, and the kind of compassion the gospel invokes is a universal, indiscriminate compassion that reaches beyond the clan or the tribe to the stranger. This is clearly what Jesus had in mind when he said,

> If you love those who love you, what credit is that to you? Even "sinners" love those who love them. And if you do good to those who are good to you, what credit is that to you? Even "sinners" do that. And if you lend to those from whom you expect repayment, what credit is that to you? Even "sinners" lend to "sinners," expecting to be repaid in full. But love your enemies, do good to them, and lend to them without expecting to get anything back. . . . Be merciful, just as your Father is merciful. (Luke 6:32-36)

Or, as Jesus said in another place,

> When you give a luncheon or dinner, do not invite your friends, your brothers or relatives, or your rich neighbors; if you do, they may invite you back and so you will be repaid. But when you give a banquet, invite the poor, the crippled, the lame, the blind, and you will be blessed. (Luke 14:12-14)

If we ask, therefore, how those of us who work in the academy can be empowered to take seriously a diversity of human beings, it is clear that biblical faith provides supports that far transcend the supports supplied by the religion of the Republic. The religion of the Republic only affirms that "all men are created equal and are endowed with certain unalienable rights." That is a marvelous beginning and one on which Christian scholars must place an extraordinary value. But biblical religion encourages believers to make sure that the rights of *all* human beings are met, especially those whose rights are abridged by society — the poor, the disenfranchised, and the oppressed. Granted, a great many Christians fail to live up to this vision, but their failure in no way negates the power of these ideals.

Having emphasized the Christian demand for compassion, we still must acknowledge that while it is one thing to extend service and compassion to a diversity of human beings, it is quite another thing to take seriously their ideas, their cultural traditions, even their religious perspectives. This, the critics argue, is the crucial step that many Christian colleges and universities are unwilling to take.

The critics may be correct in their observation regarding some Christian institutions of higher learning. But they are wrong if they think that Christian scholars have no biblical mandate for taking seriously the ideas — even the religious perspectives — of the wide variety of people who inhabit this globe.

The plain truth is that Christians are called to take other human beings seriously. In the context of the academy, this means that we must listen carefully to their points of view, always asking what we might learn from those who come from cultural, political, and religious traditions that are different from our own. Listening does not necessarily mean agreement. But listen we must. As Christian scholars, we can do no less.

When we claim, therefore, that the Christian gospel enables us to break through our own particularities, we mean to highlight the fact that the gospel always points beyond itself, first to God and then to the neighbor. For this reason, we claim the Christian gospel as a powerful support for the life of the mind and a powerful encouragement for Christians to embrace ethnic, cultural, and religious diversity.

Two Kinds of Particularities

Since we have argued that Christians — and especially Christian scholars — must learn to break through the particularities of their faith, we now must distinguish between two kinds of particularities that Christians invariably embrace.

Denominational Particularities

On the one hand, we embrace the particularities of our respective denominational traditions. There is no way we can underestimate the importance of these particularities. At the very least, they help us to create and sustain community within the context of our denominational cultures. More than that, we sometimes embrace these kinds of particularities because we feel that Scripture mandates them. We would make a very great mistake, however, if we were to absolutize these particularities, as if they somehow stood at the core of the gospel message.

The Puritans, for example, absolutized certain forms of church organization and styles of worship. Many Protestants have absolutized the biblical text, as if the text itself ("word") were synonymous with the Christian gospel ("Word"). Some Roman Catholics have absolutized ethnic expressions of the Christian faith, while the Amish have sometimes absolutized the simple life.

Like the Puritans, my own tradition — the Churches of Christ — has sometimes absolutized forms of worship (a capella music, for example) and church organization (strictly autonomous congregations), forgetting that the gospel stands in judgment on all our efforts to implement perfect forms and structures even if we imagine those forms and structures to be biblically based.

There is still another way we might think about this problem. Some of our doctrines and traditions have the ability to point quite naturally to the gospel itself. But once we insist that our particular way of framing a given doctrine is the only legitimate way to think about that issue, at that very moment that doctrine loses its ability to point beyond itself to the gospel message. Instead, it becomes nothing more than a brittle point of denominational orthodoxy. We have already mentioned, for example, how the Lutheran scholastic theologians transformed the notion of justification by grace through faith into a badge of orthodoxy, thereby losing the very genius of that formulation.

The implications these illustrations hold for the life of the mind must be obvious. The gospel can sustain the life of the mind since the gospel always points us to the God who stands in judgment on our narrowly conceived ideologies and our rigid orthodoxies. But the ideologies and orthodoxies themselves, unless they point beyond themselves to the living God, can do little to sustain the practice of Christian higher education.

The Particularity of the Gospel and the World of Paradox

The second type of particularity that all Christians embrace is what we shall call "the particularity of the Christian gospel." At this point, the question that begs to be addressed is this: Must we break through the particularity of the Christian gospel, just as we are called to break through the particularities of our respective denominational traditions?

The First Paradox: The Incarnation

The answer to this question is "yes" and "no," precisely because the gospel offers such a stunning paradox. We find this paradox embodied especially in the person of Jesus the Christ who is, himself, the heart and soul of the Christian gospel. On the one hand, Jesus affirmed his own particularity time and again. "I am the way and the truth and the life," he said. "No one comes to the Father except through me." Indeed, he claimed to be God in the flesh. Nothing could be more particular than this. As John the beloved apostle wrote,

> In the beginning was the Word, and the Word was with God, and the Word was God. He was with God in the beginning. (John 1:1)

When we ask, therefore, if we must break through the particularity of the gospel, the answer to this point is "no," for "God was reconciling the world to himself in Christ," and God alone is the Absolute to which all other particularities inevitably point.

At the same time, the answer to our question is "yes," and this "yes" emerges from the other side of our paradox: if Jesus was fully God, he was also fully human. And as a human being, he broke through his own particularity to reveal God to the world. In this instance, then, Christians are called, not to affirm the gospel as a monument or a wall through which nothing can possibly pass, but rather as a window that opens wide onto God and through which the light and love of God might illumine the family of humankind.

What we know about Jesus the human being is simply this: as a very particular human being who walked and talked and ate and eliminated and slept and loved and wept and laughed and experienced human life to the full in every conceivable way, Jesus also pointed beyond himself to the God who was himself. This is not a contradiction in terms. It is, however, a paradox — the paradox of the incarnation.

A Second Paradox: The Servant God

Not only does the Christian gospel embrace the paradox of the incarnation, that is, the notion that God took on human flesh. It also proclaims the paradox of the servant God, that is, the notion that the regal, sovereign God of the universe took upon himself the form of a servant.

Once again, this paradox is embodied in the person of Jesus the Christ, who defined his ministry precisely in terms of outreach to those who had no other advocates. According to the biblical text, Jesus was in the synagogue in Nazareth when

> the scroll of the prophet Isaiah was handed to him. Unrolling it, he found the place were it is written, "The Spirit of the Lord is on me, because he has anointed me to preach good

news to the poor. He has sent me to proclaim freedom for the prisoners and recovery of sight for the blind, to release the oppressed, to proclaim the year of the Lord's favor."

And then, in one of the most stunning passages in the entire New Testament, Jesus told his hearers, "Today this scripture is fulfilled in your hearing" (Luke 4:17-21).

Moreover, the ministry of Jesus transcended gender, race, color, creed, and social standing. He reached out to the powerful and to the marginalized, to Jews and to Greeks, to men and to women, to slaves and to free Roman citizens, to prostitutes, to tax collectors, and to thieves. Today his compassionate concern focuses on every single person in this multicultural world in which we live: Asians and Africans, Hispanics and Native Americans, Buddhists and Hindus, Jews and Christians, men and women. When it comes to compassionate concern, Jesus leaves no one out.

When we were children, many of us learned a song that went like this:

Jesus loves the little children,
    All the children of the world;
Red and yellow, black and white,
    They are precious in His sight.
Jesus loves the little children of the world.

This means that if we ask Jesus to define for us the meaning of diversity, we must be prepared for an answer that is absolutely inclusive. In Jesus' world, all human beings are infinitely valuable. From the rich young ruler to the woman caught in adultery, Jesus took everyone he encountered with complete and radical seriousness. These are just some of the ways in which Jesus broke through his own particularity.

And so we are now left with the question: Can we serve Jesus and celebrate diversity at one and the same time? If we understand anything at all about Jesus, the question answers itself. The truth is, we cannot serve Jesus *without* serving the diversity of peoples and cultures that abound in our world.

Finally, we must ask: Why is the paradox of the servant God important for Christian scholarship? In what ways can that paradox sustain the life of the mind? It means that if we seek to be his disciples, we must break through our particularity, just as he broke through his. If we will be his disciples, he said, we will take up the cross on behalf of those around us. If we wish to save our lives, we must lose our lives in service to the neighbor. We serve him best, he explained, when we serve "the least of these" — the marginalized, the oppressed, the poor, the sick, and those in prison.

But there is more, much more. For we cannot serve other people as we should unless we take them seriously as human beings — human beings with their own unique stories, their own histories, their own cultures, and their own religious traditions. How can I serve children, for example, if I isolate myself from their presence? How can I serve the poor who populate the inner city if I am ignorant of who these people are, where they come from, what they think, and how they feel? How can I prepare to serve people of other ethnic traditions or people in other parts of the world if I know nothing of their histories, their cultural traditions, and their religious commitments?

The point is simply this: if we commit ourselves to following Jesus in service to those around us, we must take diversity seriously. This means that in the context of higher education, we must commit ourselves to teaching and learning about the diversity of peoples with whom we share this globe, and to do so in the name of Jesus — not in spite of our Christian calling, but precisely *because* of that calling.

A Third Paradox: "Simul Justus et Peccator"

Finally, the Christian gospel proclaims a third paradox that holds enormous implications for the life of the mind and the practice of higher education. Luther expressed this paradox in the phrase *simul justus et peccator,* or "simultaneously justified and a sinner."

When I was a fifth-grade child, I believed that forgiveness lasted only until my next sin, and only my next prayer could remove my condemnation. As I mentioned in the preface, because I had to cross a very busy street on the way to my elementary school, it occurred to me almost daily that I could be struck by a car and killed. So each day as I approached that busy street, I reminded myself that if I were struck by a car, I must make certain to breathe a prayer of contrition before I expired. In that way, I might enter the pearly gates. Otherwise, I had no hope. That may seem like a terribly morbid perspective for an eleven-year-old kid, but that's the way it was in my West Texas world in 1953.

Years later I discovered how mistaken that perspective was, when measured by the Christian paradox that Luther expressed in the phrase *simul justus et peccator.* For the gospel proclaims that while the Christian, like every other human being, is mired inescapably in greed and self-interest and therefore in sin, he or she is simultaneously forgiven, justified, and redeemed. As Paul affirmed in Romans 8:1, "There is now no condemnation for those who are in Christ Jesus."

Not only that, but the gospel contends that every human being is fundamentally sinful and, for that reason, no one can possibly earn a place in the kingdom of God. Justification or forgiveness is therefore by grace through faith and not by works. As Paul wrote in Galatians 2:15-16,

> We who are Jews by birth and not "Gentile sinners" know that a man is not justified by observing the law, but by faith in Jesus Christ. So we, too, have put our faith in Christ Jesus that we may be justified by faith in Christ and not by observing the law, because by observing the law no one will be justified.

Luther found this doctrine enormously liberating because it freed him to take seriously his inescapably sinful nature. Luther never took the gospel as a license to sin. But the gospel did mean that he no longer had to pretend to be a saint. For that reason, he sometimes advised his followers to "sin boldly."

The implications this notion holds for the life of the mind are staggering. While our finitude means that the Christian scholar *may well* misunderstand, miscalculate, or draw erroneous conclusions, the Christian paradox, *simul justus et peccator,* means that the Christian scholar *is freed* to do all these things. Don't misunderstand. The Christian gospel is not a license for sloppy scholarship. But it does free us to take our finitude seriously, to recognize up front that we will make mistakes and that, indeed, we may well be wrong. This recognition enables the Christian scholar to approach his or her work with humility, to confess mistakes quickly and forthrightly, and to pursue the search for truth with zeal and determination, knowing that complete and final truth lies always beyond our grasp.

Conclusions

The truth is, the Christian gospel is structured on paradox from first to last. The gospel, for example, teaches that the first shall be last and the last shall be first, that the meek shall inherit the earth, that the lowly shall be exalted while the exalted shall be brought down, and that the one who wishes to become wise must first become a fool. The Apostle Paul summarized the paradoxical structure of the Christian gospel in 1 Corinthians 1:27-28: "But God chose the foolish things of the world to shame the wise; . . . the weak things of the world to shame the strong; . . . the lowly things of this world and the despised things — and the things that are not — to nullify the things that are." This is why G. K. Chesterton claimed that the "thrilling romance of [Christian] Orthodoxy" is precisely its paradoxical quality.[5]

5. G. K. Chesterton, *Orthodoxy: The Romance of Faith* (New York: Doubleday, 1959), p. 100.

When all is said and done, the paradoxical structure of the Christian gospel invites dynamic, paradoxical thinking, precisely the kind of thinking that can sustain openness, diversity, and academic freedom. Paradoxical thinking possesses this singular capability because it allows the scholar to embrace both "yes" and "no" and to embrace these contrasting answers simultaneously. In other words, one who is at home in the world of paradox feels no compulsion to resolve every question into one simple, unambiguous answer. One who is at home in the world of paradox can live with a variety of answers, even conflicting answers, knowing that each of those conflicting answers may well be at least partly correct. The scholar who has built her life on the paradox of the Christian gospel, therefore, has the potential to become a first-rate scholar, for the world of paradox is her native air.

It is true that the religion of the Republic has helped sustain the life of the mind in the American academy for over two hundred years. But should the Christian gospel do any less? Why should anyone think that Christian scholars lack the resources to sustain the life of the mind? When Christian scholars reject diversity and shy away from asking critical questions, they witness against themselves and against the gospel they claim to represent. And they witness as well against the cause of higher learning.

Christian scholars and Christian institutions of higher learning must take seriously the religion of the Republic and the Enlightenment tradition from which it comes. More than this, they must interact with that tradition in positive ways. They must do this because Christian institutions are first of all institutions of higher learning, rooted in the democratic traditions of the Western world.

Yet, the single greatest resource available to Christian scholars and Christian institutions of higher learning is not the religion of the Republic. Rather, our single greatest resource is the Christian gospel that points beyond itself to the grace of God that has revealed itself in our Lord and Savior, Jesus Christ, and that demands that each of us reflect that grace to the neighbor. To the extent that we take seriously this Christian gospel — this "paradoxical orthodoxy"

— Christian scholars and Christian colleges and universities can indeed sustain the life of the mind.

I wish to conclude with one final observation. We emphasized in the previous chapter the ways in which Christian faith and the religion of the Republic historically have stood at odds. But there is another potential relationship that Christian faith can bear to the religion of the Republic, and that relationship is complementary, not antagonistic. In his book *The Broken Covenant*, Robert N. Bellah points out that the Enlightenment suffered from what William Blake described as "single vision." Bellah explains: "Single vision was that view of the world, propagated by what Blake saw as the infernal trio — Bacon and Newton and Locke — which depended on reason alone and felt no need of the imaginative vision long nurtured in the religious and poetic traditions of the West." Blake preferred instead what he called "twofold vision" — "the awareness that there is always more than what appears, that behind every literal fact is an unfathomable depth of implication and meaning." Bellah contends that if the Enlightenment nurtured a single vision, Christianity — along with other traditional religions — possesses the power to tap rich veins of religious imagination and, in that way, to sustain the twofold vision.[6]

Accordingly, Bellah understands the relationship between the Second Great Awakening and the Deistic founding of the American Republic rather differently than does Sidney Mead. If Mead sees only an antagonistic relationship, Bellah sees complementarity. Because the Deistic Founders rooted their vision in reason alone, Bellah contends, their language "warmed the hearts of none and by itself and unaided, it could hardly have provided the imaginative basis of a [new] national consciousness." But the Second Great Awakening filled "cold external forms . . . with a warm inner life, appropriated and impressed into the imaginative life of the people."[7]

6. Robert N. Bellah, *The Broken Covenant: American Civil Religion in Time of Trial* (Chicago: University of Chicago Press, 1992), p. 72.

7. Bellah, *The Broken Covenant*, p. 45.

It is precisely this sort of relationship between reason and imagination that Christian scholars — indeed, scholars with roots in any great religious tradition — are uniquely positioned to cultivate. Here we find one of the greatest gifts that Christian scholars can bring to the life of the mind.

In the next chapter we will explore some specific Christian traditions and ask about the ways in which those traditions can sustain the life of the mind.

CHAPTER FOUR

The Power of Christian Traditions

H OW IS IT POSSIBLE FOR CHRISTIAN COLLEGES AND UNIVERSI-
ties to mature into first-rate institutions of higher learning
while, at the same time, living out of the faith traditions that gave
them birth? In the field of Christian higher education, no question
could be more urgent. Throughout the course of Western history,
numerous institutions of higher learning originally founded to serve
both the life of the mind and the Christian faith have sloughed off
their Christian underpinnings as part of their attempt to become ac-
ademically respectable.

This pattern does not imply that Christian faith and the life of
the mind are fundamentally incompatible. But it does suggest that
Christian educators have often failed to ask in meaningful ways,
"What is there in the Christian faith that can sustain serious intellectual inquiry and the life of the mind?"

We are not asking, "How is it possible for Christian faith and the
life of the mind to merely coexist?" If we frame the question in those
terms, we are beaten before we begin, for if we ask about mere coexistence, we confess — quite wrongly, I believe — that Christian faith
and serious intellectual inquiry are not compatible. If we frame the
question in terms of coexistence, therefore, we have set ourselves up
for failure and can surely anticipate that when our institutions
achieve the levels of academic excellence toward which they aspire,
their faith dimensions will inevitably wither.

We are not asking, then, about mere coexistence. Instead, we are asking how we can genuinely *live out of* our faith commitments. Put another way, is it possible to use the faith commitments of our colleges and universities as the *foundation* for academic growth and maturity? Or put another way still, is it possible to embrace serious intellectual inquiry precisely *because of* our Christian commitments, not *in spite of* those commitments?

I am convinced that the Christian faith can indeed sustain the kind of work in which Christian scholars are engaged. But for that to happen, each Christian scholar must begin to ask in a careful and systematic way, "What is there about the Christian faith, what is there about my own faith tradition, or traditions with which I am acquainted, that can genuinely sustain the life of the mind?"

We must now explore that question with reference to the Roman Catholic tradition, on the one hand, and the three great Reformation traditions, on the other: Reformed, Anabaptist, and Lutheran.

A Roman Catholic Model

When we ask how the Roman Catholic tradition can sustain the life of the mind, the first thing we must notice is the diversity that characterizes Catholic institutions of higher learning. After all, Catholic colleges and universities were established not by the church *per se* but by a variety of religious orders that bring to the task of higher education a diversity of emphases. Nonetheless, we find in all Catholic colleges and universities certain uniquely Catholic dimensions that can sustain the life of the mind.

The first characteristic of the Catholic tradition to which we should point is its *rich intellectual heritage.* The truth is, the Catholic intellectual heritage is so vast, so deep, and so broad that many Catholic intellectuals may find it strange to ask, "How can Christian faith sustain the life of the mind?" From Justin to Augustine to Lonergan, from Origen to Anselm to Teilhard, from Aquinas to Newman to

Küng, one finds here a stunning array of intellectual resources to which, in fact, no other Christian tradition in the Western world can compare.[1] As Notre Dame's James Turner has written,

> We are talking, after all, about nearly two thousand years of human intellectual effort, of grappling with the problems of human psychology, social organization, political power, and aesthetic imagination, of thinking and writing by some enormously gifted people, including at least two individuals, Augustine and Aquinas, who rank among the most profound, prolific, and creative minds of all eras.

But the most striking aspect of the Catholic intellectual heritage is its rich diversity. As Turner notes,

> This is no simple corpus; it is rife with disputation, disagreement, development, divergence. Heterogeneity and many-sidedness are among the great strengths of the Catholic intellectual traditions, one of the reasons why they have provided such rich resources for human reflection, so flexible and open-ended a source of possibilities for understanding.[2]

In this context, Protestants who imagine that faith/learning integration is a contemporary Protestant project are simply mistaken. Instead, the most widely applied program for integrating faith and learning in twentieth-century America was the Neoscholastic revival that did so much to shape Catholic higher education from the 1920s into the 1960s.[3]

1. Pope John Paul II both celebrates and seeks to extend the Catholic intellectual tradition in his encyclical letter, *Fides et Ratio* (Boston: Pauline Books and Media, 1998).

2. James Turner, "Catholic Intellectual Traditions and Contemporary Scholarship," a pamphlet published by the Cushwa Center for the Study of American Catholicism, University of Notre Dame, pp. 10 and 5.

3. On the Neoscholastic revival, see Philip Gleason, *Contending with Moder-*

If we ask about specific theological motifs that can nurture the life of the mind, the *sacramental principle* looms large in importance. This venerable Catholic doctrine points to the fact that the natural world and even elements of human culture can serve as vehicles by which God mediates his grace to human beings. This conviction allows Catholic educators to take the world seriously on its own terms and to interact with the world as it is.

If, as we shall see, some Protestant educators argue that the world and the contents of human culture are fundamentally secular if not brought under the sovereign sway of the Lord Jesus Christ, many Catholic educators, affirming the sacramental principle, take sharp issue with that contention. Alice Gallin, former executive director of the Association for Catholic Colleges and Universities, for example, has argued that "'secular' is not simply nor always the opposite of 'sacred,' for in a Christian sacramental view of reality, the secular has a legitimate role and one that is congruent with and not opposed to faith or religion."[4]

This is why David O'Brien of the College of the Holy Cross points to one of the documents of Vatican II, *The Pastoral Constitution on the Church and the Modern World,* as a virtual "magna carta" for Catholic colleges and universities. It functions in this way, O'Brien argues, since it affirms "the study of the human sciences, respect for non-Catholic, secular culture, dialogue with those beyond the church, and service to society," all in the context of the sacramental principle.[5] Two other Catholic educators — Emmanuel Renner and Hilary Thimmesh, writing in *Models for Christian Higher Education* — argue that "secularization could very well mean

nity: *Catholic Higher Education in the Twentieth Century* (New York: Oxford University Press, 1995), pp. 105-23.

4. Alice Gallin, "American Church Related Higher Education: Comparison and Contrast," ACHE presentation, December 29, 1992, p. 1.

5. David O'Brien, *From the Heart of the American Church: Catholic Higher Education and American Culture* (Maryknoll, N.Y.: Orbis, 1994), p. 49.

sacramentalization to those who recognized the presence of God in the world."[6]

In a word, the sacramental principle sustains the life of the mind by placing a very great value both on the natural world and on human culture, and by reminding us that these realms possess their own intrinsic legitimacy, whether transformed by the rule of Christ or not.

The sacramental principle does not imply that the Roman Catholic tradition possesses no serious doctrine of sin, for of course it does. Nor does it deny the possibility of genuine secularization. But it does maintain that one may well find the presence of God both in the created order and in the contents of human culture. For that reason, the notion of an inevitable slippery slope to secularization makes far less sense in a Roman Catholic context than might be the case in some other Christian traditions.

The third characteristic that allows the Catholic tradition to sustain the life of the mind is *the universality of the Catholic faith.* As a global church, Catholicism embraces believers from every corner of the world — people who hold a variety of political ideologies, who speak a myriad of tongues, who represent virtually every nationality in the world, and who reflect every social and economic class on the planet today.

The universality of the Catholic tradition *should* permit the Catholic university to prize pluralism and diversity and to find a legitimate place at the table for every conversation partner. Many have argued this case, but no one has done so more effectively than Fr. Theodore Hesburgh, president emeritus of the University of Notre Dame. "The Catholic university," Hesburgh writes,

6. Emmanuel Renner and Hilary Thimmesh, "Faith and Learning at the College of Saint Benedict and Saint John's University," in *Models for Christian Higher Education,* ed. Richard T. Hughes and William B. Adrian (Grand Rapids: Eerdmans, 1997), p. 37.

must be a *bridge* across all the chasms that separate modern people from each other: the gaps between young and old, men and women, rich and poor, black and white, believer and unbeliever, potent and weak, east and west, material and spiritual, scientist and humanist, developed and less developed, and all the rest. To be such a mediator, the Catholic university, as universal, must be engaged with, and have an interest in, both edges of every gulf, must understand each, encompass each in its total community and build a bridge of understanding and love.[7]

Indeed, the University of Notre Dame grounds its commitment to diversity and inclusion precisely in its theological tradition. Accordingly, the officers of the university released in 1997 the following statement, which now appears in all major university publications.

The University of Notre Dame strives for a spirit of inclusion among the members of this community for distinct reasons articulated in our Christian tradition. We prize the uniqueness of all persons as God's creatures. We welcome all people, regardless of color, gender, religion, ethnicity, sexual orientation, social or economic class, and nationality, for example, precisely because of Christ's calling to treat others as we desire to be treated.

Finally, we must consider a theme that Monika Hellwig describes as *the communitarian nature of redemption*. At its core, this notion holds that the church is not simply the hierarchical magisterium; instead, the church is comprised of *all* the people of God, scattered throughout the world, who together form this commu-

---

7. Theodore Hesburgh, "The Challenge and Promise of a Catholic University," in *The Challenge and Promise of a Catholic University*, ed. Hesburgh (Notre Dame: University of Notre Dame Press, 1994), pp. 9-11.

nity of faith. This means that the life of the mind, if understood only in cognitive terms, is less than adequate in a Catholic university. Instead, as Hellwig notes, the life of the mind must translate itself into

> genuine bonds of friendship and mutual respect and support [which] are envisaged as the core of the educational enterprise, because not only book learning but human formation for leadership and responsibility in all walks of life are sought through the community experience of higher education.[8]

Precisely because it takes "seriously the unity of the human race," the communitarian dimension suggests that faculties in Catholic colleges and universities should place scholarship and teaching in the service of justice and peace for all the peoples of the world. To a very great extent, many Catholic institutions have done just that. As David O'Brien observes, "president after president [in the world of Catholic higher education] has repeated the words of the American bishops insisting that pursuit of justice and human dignity is an essential work of a Catholic institution."[9]

It is clear that the Roman Catholic tradition is at home with human reason, with the natural world, with secular human culture, with human history, with human beings who stand both inside and outside of the Catholic faith, and with human beings in every conceivable social circumstance. It is precisely this dimension that renders the Catholic faith, at least in theory, so compatible with the ideals of the modern university.

At the same time, it is entirely possible for the Catholic tradition to stand at odds with the life of the mind. This can happen when dogmatism displaces inquiry, when a rigid orthodoxy undermines

8. Monika Hellwig, "What Can the Roman Catholic Tradition Contribute to Christian Higher Education?" in *Models,* ed. Hughes and Adrian, p. 21.

9. O'Brien, *From the Heart of the American Church,* pp. 86-87.

the search for truth, when Catholics so completely identify their heritage of faith with particular ethnic or nationalist traditions that they fail to embrace the universal dimensions of their own tradition, or when Catholics absolutize those dimensions of their faith that might otherwise have the potential to break through their own particularity.

A Reformed Model

On the Protestant side of the ledger, we begin with the Reformed tradition since that model is so widely known and embraced in so many Protestant circles of church-related higher education. Admittedly, the Reformed tradition today is hardly monolithic, embracing as it does a variety of Presbyterian denominations, a variety of Dutch Reformed denominations, and several other communions — including the Southern Baptist Convention — that descend in one way or another from the work of John Calvin.

But in the world of Reformed Christianity, only one tradition has developed a thoroughgoing understanding of how Christian faith can sustain the life of the mind. For that reason, the following description will focus especially on a theoretical understanding that has its deepest roots at Calvin College in Grand Rapids, Michigan, an institution related to the Christian Reformed Church.[10] Though birthed at Calvin College, this vision has subsequently exerted an extraordinary impact on evangelical Protestant colleges and universities throughout the country.

If we ask, "In what ways can the Reformed tradition sustain the life of the mind?" the answer has everything to do with the original

10. Calvin College issued an important statement on the meaning of Christian education in the Reformed genre in *Christian Liberal Arts Education: Report of the Calvin College Curriculum Study Committee* (Grand Rapids: Calvin College and Eerdmans Publishing Co., 1970).

vision of John Calvin. Simply put, Calvin sought to transform Geneva, Switzerland, into a model kingdom of God. To achieve this goal, he sought to place every facet of Genevan life — its religion, its politics, its music, and its art — squarely under the sovereignty of God. Ever since those early days, this same vision has motivated Calvinists to bring all human life and culture under the sovereign sway of God's control. Abraham Kuyper, the Dutch statesman and philosopher, expressed this vision well: "There is not a square inch on the whole plane of human existence over which Christ, who is Lord over all, does not proclaim: 'This is Mine!'"[11]

If all of this sounds terribly theocratic, we must also recall that the doctrine of the sovereignty of God can also move in very democratic directions. For example, the early French Calvinist Philip Mornay appealed to this doctrine in his attempt to undermine the absolute power of kings and place power in the hands of the people. Likewise, it is no accident that the vast majority of the American patriots who sought to resist the tyranny of King George III were Calvinists who firmly believed that if God alone is sovereign, no human being has the right to tyrannize his or her fellow mortals.

Still, in the world of Reformed Christianity, the doctrine of the sovereignty of God often finds expression in the attempt to transform human culture into the kingdom of God on earth. This is precisely the vision that sustains the life of the mind in places like Calvin College and in the various evangelical institutions that Calvin College has influenced. Educators who rely on this vision seek to place the entire curriculum — and every course within the curriculum — under the sovereignty of God. According to this vision, all learning should be Christian in both purpose and orientation. For this reason, Reformed educators employ three fundamental concepts that underscore these objectives.

11. Abraham Kuyper, "Souvereiniteit in Eigen Kring" (Amsterdam: Kruyt, 1880), p. 32, cited in James D. Bratt and Ronald A. Wells, "Piety and Progress: A History of Calvin College," in *Models,* ed. Hughes and Adrian, p. 143.

The first and most important of those concepts is a notion popularized by Kuyper, the notion of a *Christian worldview*. As Albert Wolters points out, Kuyper argued that "Calvinism was not just a theology or a system of ecclesiastical polity but a complete worldview with implications for all of life, implications which must be worked out and applied in such areas as politics, art, and scholarship." With such a worldview, Kuyper believed, Christianity could provide broad cultural leadership in the nineteenth century and compete head to head with other perspectives like socialism or Darwinism or positivism.[12] With their insistence on a Christian worldview, Reformed educators contributed to the world of higher education an awareness of the power of presuppositions long before the rise of postmodernist theory.

Central to the notion of a Christian worldview stands the second conviction, the notion that *all truth is God's truth*. By this phrase, Reformed educators mean to say that God is the author not only of our faith, but also of every facet of the world in which we live. If this is true, they insist, then there can be no discrepancy between Christian convictions and authentic knowledge regarding other aspects of human life. It is therefore possible to understand every facet of the natural sciences, of the social sciences, and of religion and the humanities in the light of Christian faith without running the risk of intellectual dishonesty.

It is precisely this conviction that breathes life into the third concept employed by Reformed educators: *the integration of faith and learning*. Because all truth is God's truth, all learning should be integrated into a coherent understanding of reality, informed by explicitly Christian convictions. No one has expressed the theological rationale for this perspective better than Arthur Holmes in his classic book, *The Idea of a Christian College*. There Holmes argues,

---

12. Albert Wolters, "On the Idea of Worldview and Its Relation to Philosophy," in *Stained Glass: Worldviews and Social Science,* ed. Paul A. Marshall, Sander Griffioen, and Richard J. Mouw (Lanham, Md.: University Press of America, 1989), p. 20.

When the apostle writes that in Christ "are hid all the trea-
sures of wisdom and knowledge" (Col. 2:3), he refers . . . to
[the fact that] Jesus Christ is . . . Creator and Lord of every
created thing. All our knowledge of anything comes into focus around that fact. We see nature, persons, society, and the
arts and sciences in proper relationship to their divine Creator and Lord. . . . The truth is a coherent whole by virtue of
the common focus that ties it all into one.[13]

It is incumbent, therefore, upon Reformed educators to integrate explicitly Christian convictions into every branch of learning and,
more than that, to discover those common, Christocentric threads
that transform all fields of learning into one coherent whole.[14]

Finally, this triad of ideas — *a Christian worldview, all truth is
God's truth,* and *the integration of faith and learning* — sustains another notion that is critical to at least one version of the Reformed
understanding of reality: the notion of *secularization.* One finds in
the Reformed tradition two perspectives on this theme. First, Calvin
himself argued that "the Spirit of God [is] the sole fountain of
truth," whether one finds that truth in the secular sphere or in divine
revelation.[15] Extending this line of thought, many Calvinists today
argue for a doctrine of "common grace." According to this under-

13. Arthur Holmes, *The Idea of a Christian College,* rev. ed. (Grand Rapids:
Eerdmans, 1987), p. 17.

14. While many Reformed scholars employ the "integration of faith and learning" language, not every Reformed thinker agrees with this formulation. For example, Carl E. Zylstra, president of Dordt College in Iowa, argues that the language of
"integration" implies an artificial connectedness. What is needed, he suggests, is
language that conveys the real objective of Reformed education, namely, *rooting*
learning in Christian faith. For this reason, he suggests the phrase "faith-based
learning" as a preferable ideal. "Faith-Based Learning: The Conjunction in Christian Scholarship," *Pro Rege* 26 (September 1997): 1-5.

15. John Calvin, *Institutes of the Christian Religion,* 2.2.15, ed. John T. McNeill,
trans. Ford Lewis Battles, The Library of Christian Classics, vol. 20 (Philadelphia:
Westminster, 1960), pp. 273-75.

standing, God sustains a significant measure of truth, beauty, and justice, even in the midst of a fallen and secularized world.

At the same time, following another impulse in Calvin, many contemporary Reformed thinkers view the secular as a hindrance to the Christian presence in the world and therefore seek to overcome it by transforming it into the kingdom of God.[16] From this perspective, secularization occurs when there is even one dimension of human life that escapes the sovereignty of God, or when we fail to bring all of reality under the umbrella of a distinctly Christian worldview. Because the possibility of secularization is so real in this context, the notion of a *slippery slope* is a metaphor that many in this tradition take very seriously. If one hopes to avoid the slippery slope toward secularization, therefore, the integration of faith and learning around a distinctly Christian worldview becomes absolutely imperative.

This aspect of the Reformed tradition stands in stark relief when we compare it with Lutheranism, on the one hand, and Catholicism, on the other. For if some in the Reformed tradition argue that the slippery slope to secularization is a real and present danger, many in the Lutheran and Catholic traditions acknowledge that the secular can often serve as a legitimate vehicle of the grace of God.

Clearly, the Reformed tradition sustains the life of the mind by integrating faith and learning around a distinctly Christian worldview. One can identify at least three great strengths of this perspective, whether one subscribes to the Reformed worldview or not. First, it overcomes fragmentation with its holistic approach to learning. Second, it frankly acknowledges the reality and power of worldviews and presuppositions. And third, it provides students with a clearly defined standpoint from which they can discriminate between competing perspectives and worldviews. And if one cares about relating faith to learning at all, one is likely to find the Re-

16. See Nicholas Wolterstorff's important discussion of the role of the secular in Reformed thought in *Until Justice and Peace Embrace* (Grand Rapids: Eerdmans, 1983), pp. 12 and 40-41.

formed emphasis on the sovereignty of God over the entire learning process extraordinarily compelling.

But to what extent does the Reformed perspective encourage academic freedom and genuine interaction with pluralism and diversity?[17] Put another way, to what extent does the Reformed tradition encourage the scholar to break through the particularity of his or her own religious vision and to engage other visions in serious and compelling ways?

There are two answers to that question. First, if a given scholar embraces the Reformed worldview, and is willing to understand all reality from the standpoint of that perspective, she or he will experience substantial academic freedom. Arthur Holmes, among others, has made this point abundantly clear.

> Academic freedom is valuable only when there is a prior commitment to the truth. And commitment to the truth is fully worthwhile only when that truth exists in One who transcends both the relativity of human perspectives and the fears of human concern.[18]

On the other hand, while the Reformed perspective allows the scholar substantial freedom to search for penultimate truths within the context of an all-embracing Christian worldview, the Reformed perspective is always susceptible to the twin risks of triumphalism and distortion. A hypothetical case in point might be a class in world religions. If, for example, one were to study Buddhism from the standpoint of a Christian worldview, one might easily run the risk of distorting Buddhism into something it is not or debunking Buddhism in favor of a triumphalist Christian perspective.

17. For a superb discussion of the question of academic freedom within a Reformed context, see Anthony J. Diekema, *Academic Freedom & Christian Scholarship* (Grand Rapids: Eerdmans, 2000).

18. Holmes, *The Idea of a Christian College*, p. 69.

And yet, the Reformed tradition contains at its core a powerful sentiment that can undermine triumphalism. That sentiment is simply the historic Reformed insistence on the finitude of humankind and of all human thinking and constructions. Arthur Holmes points squarely to that conviction when he writes, "Truth is not yet fully known; every academic discipline is subject to change, correction, and expansion — even theology." Holmes further notes that even worldview construction must take on tentative dimensions. A Christian worldview, he argues, is merely "exploratory, not a closed system worked out once and for all but an endless undertaking. . . . It remains open-ended because the task is so vast that to complete it would require the omniscience of God."[19]

And yet, the notion that God has called upon his saints to renovate the world is such an overpowering theme in the Reformed tradition that the profoundly Calvinist theme of human finitude and brokenness can sometimes get lost in the shuffle.

A Mennonite Model

When we turn from the Reformed to the Anabaptist/Mennonite tradition, we quickly discover that we have entered into a frame of reference radically different from the Reformed perspective. The first thing we notice is that the starting point for Mennonites has more to do with holistic living than with cognition and more to do with ethics than with intellect. One faculty member at Goshen College, a Mennonite college in Indiana, summarized very nicely the difference between the Reformed and Mennonite models when she observed that if the Reformed model is fundamentally cerebral and transforms living by thinking, the Mennonite model transforms thinking by living.

This vision represents a challenge to those who think of higher

19. Holmes, *The Idea of a Christian College*, pp. 58-59 and 66.

learning exclusively in cerebral terms. Perhaps for that reason, critics have suggested that the Mennonite tradition offers no serious model for developing the enterprise of Christian higher education. A few years ago, I spoke on the campus of a midwestern church-related college on the topic, "Models for Christian Higher Education." I described my conception of a Catholic model, a Lutheran model, a Reformed model, and finally a Mennonite model for the task of Christian higher education. When I finished my presentation, a gentleman noted for his rigorous scholarship rose to ask, "Why do you speak of a Mennonite model? Mennonites have no serious model at all." Months later, another critic of the Mennonite tradition shared with me his conviction that education is primarily a matter of the head. "But Mennonites," he lamented, "focus on hands and heart."

Mennonites do indeed "focus on hands and heart," but instead of constituting a liability, this emphasis is one of their greatest strengths. For when Mennonites "focus on hands and heart," they remind us that human life is more than cognition. They therefore help us to see that higher education in the Christian genre must be multifaceted and holistic, helping students to develop every aspect of their being, not simply their minds.

Yet, if we assume that by focusing on hands and heart, Mennonites neglect the life of the mind, we are badly mistaken. Mennonites prize the life of the mind, but they rarely divorce cognition from lifestyle commitments, grounded in Christian faith. More precisely, Mennonites begin their task by seeking to implement a vision of discipleship that takes its cue from the radical teachings of Jesus. They take seriously Jesus' words when he counseled his followers to abandon self in the service of others and especially in the service of the poor, or when he charged his disciples to practice humility, simplicity, and nonviolence. Theirs is a radical vision, to be sure, and one that stands almost entirely out of sync with the values of the larger culture.

One who is not accustomed to the Mennonite frame of reference might well ask what this perspective has to do with the life of the mind. How can unconventional virtues like these possibly sustain the values we associate with the academy? Put another way, how does one move from Christocentric living to critical and pluralistic thinking?

We can answer that question in four ways. First, we must recall that sixteenth-century Anabaptism originated in the very womb of dissent. For well over a thousand years, Europeans had taken for granted the notion of a state church. No one could imagine a stable society without it. And the one rite that maintained the state church was the sacrament of infant baptism. For hundreds of years since the days of Theodosius the Great in the late fourth century, every infant had been baptized within days of its birth, and in that way every child — and as a result, every person in society — was both citizen and Christian. Church and state were virtually coterminous.

The problem was one of commitment. How could one speak of discipleship in a church that embraced not only saints, but also thieves, murderers, liars, adulterers, and those who had no serious concern with Christian faith at all? This was the problem that became inescapably clear to a small group of men and women in Zurich, Switzerland, in the early 1520s. These people had read the New Testament and understood full well the radical teachings of Jesus. They therefore longed for a church composed only of people willing to commit themselves to lives of radical discipleship. But this would mean the rejection of infant baptism in favor of the baptism of believing adults.

The Zurich city council discussed this proposal, but finally rejected it with the following affirmation:

> Therefore all those who have recently left their children unbaptized must have them baptized within eight days. Whoever does not want to do this must leave our town, jurisdiction and domain with his wife, children and property, or await further action against him.

Undaunted, a small group of dissenters met in the home of Felix Manz on January 21, 1525. Their position was both simple and clear: they must obey God rather than men. Accordingly,

> After the prayer, George Cajacob arose and asked Conrad [Grebel] to baptize him, for the sake of God, with the true Christian baptism upon his faith and knowledge. And when he knelt down with that request and desire, Conrad baptized him. . . .

Following his baptism, George of the House of Jacob baptized all the others present. In that way, the Anabaptist movement was begun. As the *Hutterite Chronicle* notes, "Therewith began the separation from the world and its evil works."

The Zurich city council responded quickly. On March 7, 1526, the council proclaimed, "Whoever hereafter baptizes someone will be apprehended by our Lords and, according to this present decree, be drowned without mercy."[20] Within a few years, virtually everyone who had met in Felix Manz's home on the night of January 21, 1525, had been executed. The repression quickly spread. Catholics, Lutherans, Zwinglians, and Calvinists all agreed that seditious and heretical people like these deserved extermination. Accordingly, thousands of Anabaptists met their deaths over the next ten to fifteen years. They were burned at the stake, run through by the sword, hanged, or tied in bags and dumped into the sea, accompanied by the taunt, "Here is your water, Anabaptist!"

I have told this story for one reason: In a world that prized lockstep uniformity, Anabaptists dared to question the status quo, and they paid for their convictions with their lives. It matters little that their dissent began with commitments of the heart, not with

---

20. All these citations may be found in *The Reformation: A Narrative History Related by Contemporary Observers and Participants,* ed. Hans Hillerbrand (New York: Harper and Row, 1964), pp. 230-33.

high-level theoretical formulations. Regardless of their starting point, sixteenth-century Anabaptists proved time and again their commitment to independent thinking. If a willingness to question conventional wisdom stands at the heart of the academic enterprise, then surely the Anabaptist heritage offers important resources for sustaining the life of the mind.

Second, Mennonites routinely counsel one another to abandon self in the interest of others and to abandon narrow nationalism in the interest of world citizenship. For this reason, service to other human beings, especially to the poor, the marginalized, and the oppressed throughout the world, stands at the heart of the Mennonite witness. If we ask how a global service commitment like this can sustain the life of the mind, the answer is not hard to find. It is difficult to abandon self for the sake of others in any meaningful sense unless one is prepared to take seriously those "others," their cultural contexts, and their points of view. This means that Mennonite colleges, precisely because of their service orientation, are prepared to take seriously one of the cardinal virtues of the modern academy: the emphasis on pluralism and diversity.

If one wishes to see how this commitment might play itself out in an academic context, one need only consider the international studies program at Goshen College, where 80 percent of all students spend an entire semester in a third-world culture, serving and seeking to learn that country's history, traditions, and language.

Third, the Mennonite heritage offers its scholars an extraordinary basis from which to engage in critical thinking. The ability to engage in critical thinking depends on two factors. First, it requires a perspective or vantage point from which one can make critical and discriminating judgments. Second, one's frame of reference must be vulnerable to criticism even as the scholar employs that frame of reference as a basis for critiquing other perspectives. Put another way, one must have a place to stand, but at the same time, one must be able to break through the particularity of one's own intellectual foundation.

In the Mennonite tradition, the vantage point that allows one to make discriminating judgments is not a theological abstraction. Rather, it is a story-formed community. Story plays a powerful role in the Mennonite tradition. The story with which Mennonites most identify is the story of the "little flock," the persecuted remnant, beginning with Stephen, the first Christian martyr, continuing through the history of the ancient and medieval periods, and finally erupting into a massive persecution of believers in the sixteenth century. Nor is this story a disembodied tale, passed down by oral tradition alone. Instead, it became incarnate in book form in 1660 when Thieleman J. van Braght released his *Bloody Theater or Martyrs Mirror of the Defenseless Christians, Who Baptized Only Upon Confession of Faith . . . , From the Time of Christ to the Year A.D. 1660.*[21] Around this concept of the "little flock," Mennonites have built an extraordinary sense of community.

A story-formed community like this one could easily nurture a spirit of tribalism and thereby preclude critical thinking. In all honesty, we must admit that this is precisely what happens in some Mennonite and Amish circles. But the genius of the Mennonite story lies in its outward orientation. In other words, Mennonites remember what it means to be a persecuted remnant, but they also remember the commitments that brought on the persecutions: the embrace of nonresistance, the rejection of materialism, the commitment to the poor, and the passion to emulate Jesus in his ministry to "the least of these." So long as this story-formed community reaches beyond itself to the stranger, to men and women of other cultures and other faith traditions, to orphans and widows and the despised of the earth — so long as this is true, the Mennonite story is a dialectical story. This story affirms a specific faith tradition — but precisely because of that tradition, the Mennonite story reaches beyond itself to men and women who tell stories completely different from the

21. Thieleman J. van Braght, *The Bloody Theater or Martyrs Mirror*, trans. Joseph F. Sohm (Scottdale, Pa.: Herald Press, 1950).

story celebrated in *The Martyrs Mirror.* For this reason, the Mennonite tradition holds the potential to nurture critical thinking in extraordinary ways.

Finally, because of its historic emphasis on humility, the Mennonite tradition prepares its scholars to embrace one of the cardinal virtues of the academic guild: the willingness to admit that my understandings are fragmentary and incomplete and that, indeed, I could be wrong.

For all these reasons, the Mennonite commitment to a life of radical discipleship can contribute in substantial ways to a vigorous life of the mind. Yet, we must also acknowledge that while the Mennonite commitment to stand with a radical Jesus is surely one of their greatest strengths, it can also be a serious liability in the arena of higher education. Ironically, the very commitment that has often inspired humility, dissent, and respect for cultural diversity can also inspire narrowness and sectarian exclusivity. This can happen in several ways. It can happen, for example, when Mennonites allow the radical teachings of Jesus to become little more than the substance of ethnic folkways, or when they take seriously the ethical mandates of Jesus without embracing with equal seriousness the grace of God whereby he forgives us *in spite of* our failings and shortcomings.

A Lutheran Model

We now must ask, "What resources does the Lutheran tradition offer for sustaining the life of the mind?" I want to begin this exploration by recalling two comments made to me by two different Lutheran professors in two different schools. A Lutheran teaching in a Reformed institution remarked, "When I first came to this school, I couldn't hook onto this 'worldview' business that everyone talked about. At first I thought I was dumb. I finally decided I was just Lutheran." A second person — this time a Lutheran teaching at a Lutheran institution — spoke of how exhausting it was to teach in a

Lutheran context. When I asked why, he spoke of the constant interplay and tension he felt between the sacred and the secular. These two comments offer telling clues to the rich resources for sustaining the life of the mind that reside in the Lutheran heritage.

The first resource the Lutheran tradition offers for sustaining the life of the mind is Luther's insistence on human finitude and the sovereignty of God. But having made that affirmation, we must also recognize that Lutheran theology is not a static and self-contained orthodoxy that simply stands there, gazing at itself in all its narcissistic splendor. Nor is Lutheran theology linear or flat or one-dimensional. Nor can we rightly regard Luther's theology as an orthodoxy at all if we understand the word "orthodoxy" in its conventional sense. Instead, Luther offers us a dynamic and vibrant vision, always subverting any confidence we may have in our own ability to do the good, to tell the truth, or to get the story right in any full or final sense.

To speak of human finitude, then, is to point not only to our frailties and limitations or our estrangement from God, from other human beings, and even from ourselves; it also points to the depth and breadth of sin that undermines our ability to fully grasp or do the good. When Luther argues for God's sovereignty, therefore, his point is not that Christians should impose God's sovereignty on an unbelieving world. That would be an impossible absurdity. Rather, when Luther points to God's sovereignty, he always points at the very same time to human finitude. The sovereignty of God, therefore, means that I am not God, that my reason is inevitably impaired, and that my knowledge is always fragmentary and incomplete.

In the context of higher education and the life of the mind, this position means that every scholar must always confess that he or she could be wrong. Apart from this confession, there can be no serious life of the mind, for only when we confess that we might be wrong can we engage in the kind of conversation that takes seriously other voices. And only when we confess that we might be wrong are we empowered to assess in critical ways our own theories, our own judgments, and our own understandings.

§   *The Vocation of the Christian Scholar*

This does not mean that we have no confidence in what we know. We do indeed have confidence in what we know since we are made in the image of God. At the same time, our confidence must be tentative, not absolute, since we are victims of sin and the fall. Put another way, in the Lutheran tradition, doubt is always the partner of faith. In his marvelous book, *Exiles from Eden,* Mark Schwehn quotes James Gustafson to the effect that "we believe what we question and question what we believe."[22] Or, as the father of the boy with the evil spirit confessed to Jesus in Mark 9, "Lord, I believe; help thou mine unbelief." In the Lutheran context, one who refuses to confess that he or she might be wrong has forfeited the ability to engage in critical scholarship and really has no legitimate place in the academy.

Because of the Lutheran insistence on human finitude, Lutheran theology always has the capacity to break through its own particularity. Authentic Lutherans can never absolutize their own perspectives, even their theological perspectives. They must always be reassessing and rethinking, and they must always be in dialogue with themselves and with others.

But there is more, for if Lutherans *must* always be in dialogue with themselves and with others, it is equally true to say that they are *free* to be in dialogue with themselves and with others. For knowledge that one is justified by grace through faith grants the Christian scholar a profound sense of freedom to question his or her own best insights, to revise them, or to discard them and start again. This is the genius of the Lutheran tradition, and this is the first reason why the Lutheran worldview can sustain the life of the mind.

The second resource the Lutheran tradition offers for sustaining the life of the mind is Luther's notion of paradox, a theme that stands at the heart of Lutheran thought. Luther prized the theme of paradox, not because the notion of paradox was philosophically in-

22. Mark Schwehn, *Exiles from Eden: Religion and the Academic Vocation in America* (Oxford: Oxford University Press, 1993), p. 49.

triguing, but rather because he found the notion of paradox at the very heart of the Christian gospel. Indeed, the notion of paradox is deeply embedded in Luther's "theology of the cross." In this upside-down world of redemption, life emerges from the throes of death, the first are last and the last are first, and the Christian is the one who is simultaneously justified and a sinner. Because his "theology of the cross" stands at the very center of Luther's thought, so does the notion of paradox.

Of all the paradoxes that abound in the Lutheran vision, there is none more supportive of the life of the mind than Luther's notion of the two kingdoms. In his view, the Christian lives in the world and in the kingdom of God — or, put another way, in nature and in grace — and does so simultaneously. In fact, in Luther's vision, God employs the finite dimensions of the natural world as vehicles that convey his grace to human beings. As Luther often affirmed, *finitum capax infiniti,* or "the finite is the bearer of the infinite." This means that both kingdoms — the kingdom of nature and the kingdom of grace — stand under the rule of God, each in its own way.

Precisely for this reason, Luther suggested that the distinction we often wish to make between the sacred and secular spheres may be fraught with far more ambiguity than we may wish to admit. Accordingly, Luther wrote in his 1520 treatise, "The Freedom of the Christian,"

> It does not help the soul if the body is adorned with the sacred robes of priests or dwells in sacred places or is occupied with sacred duties or prays, fasts, abstains from certain kinds of foods, or does any work that can be done by the body and in the body. The righteousness and the freedom of the soul require something far different since the things which have been mentioned could be done by any wicked person. Such works produce nothing but hypocrites. On the other hand, it will not harm the soul if the body is clothed in secular dress, dwells in unconsecrated places, eats and drinks as others do, does not

pray aloud, and neglects to do all the above-mentioned things which hypocrites can do.[23]

In a word, Luther is telling us here that the sacred and secular spheres overlap in remarkable ways and simply do not conform to the neat distinctions we wish to make from our finite angle of vision. At this point, the Lutheran tradition greatly resembles Catholic sacramental understandings.

The authentic Lutheran vision, therefore, never calls for Lutherans to transform the secular world into the kingdom of God as many in the Reformed tradition have advocated over the years. Nor does it call for Lutherans to separate from the world as the heirs of the Anabaptists sometimes seek to do. Instead, the Christian must reside in two worlds at one and the same time: the world of nature and the world of grace. In Luther's view, the Christian is therefore free to take seriously *both* the secular world *and* the kingdom of God.

This notion carries great implications for the life of the mind, especially if we think of the life of the mind as one that fosters *genuine conversation* in which all the voices at the table are taken seriously. In the context of Luther's two kingdoms, there is no need to superimpose on other voices a "Christian worldview." Nor is it important to "integrate faith and learning" around a distinctly Christian perspective. Rather, one lives in the midst of a paradox in which the sacred and the secular intersect and converge. Put another way, Luther's vision sustains conversation and dialogue and resists homogeneous conformity to imperialistic understandings. Luther's notion of the two kingdoms is therefore fully capable of sustaining a commitment to the Christian faith and a serious engagement with the secular world at one and the same time. For this reason, the notion of a slippery slope to secularization scarcely makes sense in a Lutheran context.

23. Martin Luther, "Freedom of the Christian," in *Martin Luther: Selections from His Writings*, ed. John Dillenberger (New York: Doubleday, 1962), p. 54.

Yet, it may be partly misleading to speak of the notion of paradox as I have here. After reading this chapter in an earlier draft, Professor Patricia O'Connell Killen of Pacific Lutheran University wrote the following.

> It is as much if not more the quality of living in the paradox between sovereignty of God and finitude of humans that characterizes Lutheran higher education than the deductions you draw from this paradox for higher education. For example, one does not grasp once and for all Luther's insistence on human finitude and the sovereignty of God. It takes a lifetime to grasp this with one's mind, heart, will, being.

After all, Killen points out, Lutheran faith has at least as much to do with subjectivity, sensibilities, and aesthetics as it does with formal and definable intellectual content.[24] This is why we can never reduce Lutheran faith to theological formulas that can be codified intellectually and grasped in some final kind of way. And this is why it is probably inappropriate to use the Reformed language of "worldview" to describe the Lutheran theological vision.

It is precisely because Luther has such great appreciation for the depth of human finitude, because he understands the ambiguity of the human situation, and because he knows that from the perspective of the infinite, this world is full of appearances, and appearances deceive — it is for all these reasons that the Lutheran tradition possesses such an extraordinary capacity to break through its own particularity. This is why the principles of the Lutheran vision are fundamentally in keeping with the Enlightenment vision that Sidney Mead describes as the "theology of the Republic," why the Lutheran heritage can give us the courage to raise the most radical kinds of questions, and why the Lutheran vision can do so much to sustain the life of the mind.

24. Letter from Patricia O'Connell Killen to Richard Hughes, January 24, 1999.

Now we are in a position to understand why the young scholar teaching in a Lutheran institution could speak of his work in that institution as so exhausting. It *is* exhausting to constantly question your own presuppositions. It *is* exhausting to live in the midst of an unresolved tension between the sacred and the secular. And it *is* exhausting to allow the sacred and the secular to dialogue with one another in the midst of one's own work. It is far easier to assume that our presuppositions are true and right. And it is far easier to superimpose our religious perspectives on the world we seek to study.

The truth is, the Lutheran tradition possesses some of the most potent theological resources for sustaining the life of the mind that one can imagine. It encourages dialogue between the Christian faith and the world of ideas, fosters intellectual humility, engenders a healthy suspicion of absolutes, and helps create a conversation in which all conversation partners are taken seriously.

At the same time, the strength of the Lutheran tradition is also its weakness. As we have seen, Lutheran theology thrives on the theme of paradox. But it is difficult — incredibly difficult — to keep both sides of the paradox alive and to nurture each simultaneously. It is all too easy to sacrifice one side of the paradox in the interest of the other. When the paradox dissolves in this way, the risks can be absolutism on the one hand and relativism on the other.

These temptations are especially apparent when one considers Luther's understanding of the two kingdoms. If we accentuate the kingdom of God at the expense of the secular world, we run the risk of absolutizing our religious vision and imposing that vision on the world in which we live. Here one thinks, for example, of the Scholastic theologians who absolutized the dynamic, paradoxical qualities of Luther's thought into a rigid, airtight system. Or one thinks of those early Lutherans in the United States who developed a strongly catechetical form of their faith since they felt that a catechetical religion could sustain them in an alien religious culture. It is safe to say that this version of Lutheran theology is simply inimical to the life of the mind. Yet, rigid codification of Lutheran thought occurs even within some Lutheran colleges and universities.

On the other hand, if we accentuate the secular world at the expense of the kingdom of God, we run the risk of relativism. Indeed, apart from its insistence on the kingdom of God the Lutheran tradition could easily resemble a flaccid secular ideology in which nothing is ultimate, transcendent, or absolute.

The scholar who hopes to draw on the Lutheran heritage to sustain the life of the mind must therefore find ways to live out the heart and soul of Luther's original vision — a vision defined most of all by the paradox of the Christian gospel.

Looking Ahead

We now have explored four different Christian models for sustaining the life of the mind: a Catholic model, a Reformed model, an Anabaptist model, and a Lutheran model. We have discovered that each of these faith traditions has its own theological resources that can sustain the academic enterprise.

But we also must observe that none of these traditions has a monopoly on the theological motifs we have discussed. For example, while the Reformed tradition does not accentuate the notion of paradox as the Lutheran tradition does, it is nonetheless true that the seeds of paradoxical thinking — the sovereignty of God and the finitude of humankind — are fundamental to the Reformed perspective. And while Mennonites do not embrace a vision of the transformation of society as Reformed Christians do, they surely seek to transform the lives and hearts of individual men and women. Likewise, while one would hardly regard the quintessential Lutheran theme of justification by grace through faith as a defining motif of the historic Catholic tradition, that theme has nonetheless played a defining role in the thought of many Catholic theologians.

These points are important for several reasons. First, in presenting these four faith traditions, I have tried to present ideal types. But ideal types are rare in real life. More important still is the fact that many Christian institutions of higher learning — especially evangelical institutions — define themselves with reference to a variety of faith traditions and theological motifs. Even schools that are closely related to specific faith traditions often employ faculty who represent other faith perspectives.

I am therefore not suggesting that a particular theological perspective should be a unifying feature of a church-related college or university. But I am suggesting that scholars who wish to ground their scholarship in Christian convictions should pay close regard to these four great traditions of the Christian faith: Roman Catholic, Reformed, Mennonite, and Lutheran. Indeed, these four traditions complement one another in important ways, and professors who can utilize the insights of each of these traditions will enhance their teaching and scholarship immeasurably.

We now must turn our attention to a slightly different question: "What might it mean to *teach* from a Christian perspective?" Implicit in that question is another: "How can Christian scholars draw on various understandings of the Christian faith to sustain them in their classroom work?" In the following chapter, we will seek to illumine some answers to those questions.

CHAPTER FIVE

What Might It Mean to Teach from a Christian Perspective?

THROUGHOUT THIS BOOK, WE HAVE ASKED THE QUESTION, "How can Christian faith sustain the life of the mind?" Now I want to refocus that question so that it reads, "What might it mean to teach from a Christian perspective?" In this way, I will be asking, "How can Christian faith sustain the life of the mind *in the context of our classrooms?*"

To shed some light on that question, I want to use my own teaching experience as a template. In doing so, I do not by any means hold up my pedagogical practices as models that readers should emulate. But I hope that readers might find some of what follows at least suggestive.

We perhaps should confess from the outset that Christian professors wrestle with no more perplexing question than the one that frames this discussion: what might it mean to teach from a Christian perspective?

On the one hand, even though we know that perspectival teaching is inevitable, we dare not exploit that inevitability. We dare not transform our lecterns into pulpits. We must honor the values of the academy and respect the right of our students to search for truth. This side of the equation clearly calls for a mode of inquiry that refuses to shut down thought and conversation, that can live comfortably with ambiguity and disagreement, and that refuses to offer easy answers when, with our encouragement, our students might well discover answers for themselves.

At the same time, if we are Christians, we know full well that our commitment to the Christian faith inevitably lends shape and texture to all that we do, including our teaching and our scholarship. This side of the equation, then, requires from us a clear and unambiguous affirmation.

The problem for Christian professors is therefore obvious: How can we teach from a Christian perspective while honoring, at the very same time, the values and the integrity of the academy? How can we embrace these two commitments simultaneously? How can we live between the two poles of this dialectical frame of reference?

The answer begins to emerge when we recognize that Christian scholar/teachers do, in fact, live in the midst of paradox. That fact is inescapable. What we do with that paradox, then, becomes the paramount question that begs for an answer. We can repress the paradoxical qualities of our lives and our careers and hope they might go away, or we can take the reality of paradox upon ourselves and forthrightly embrace a paradoxical way of living and a paradoxical way of teaching.

That should not be such a difficult thing to do, for the model we need for paradoxical living and teaching is close at hand. In fact, it belongs to the essence of the Christian gospel. Every Christian affirms that God took on human flesh and thereby reconciled the world to himself, but we must come to see what a remarkable paradox this is. Every Christian believes that we are justified by grace through faith, in spite of the incredible depth and breadth of our sin. But when we make this claim, we affirm a paradox that shatters reason and destroys every attempt to frame Christian faith in simple, linear terms. Every Christian believes that though we are in the world, we are not of the world, but not every Christian recognizes the incredible paradox involved in that assertion.

The truth is, Christian faith is built on a paradoxical framework at every crucial turn, and if we seek to reduce the Christian religion to a set of simple, linear statements that have no paradoxical qualities about them whatsoever, then we have robbed the Christian faith of its power to sustain the life of the mind.

If we wish, therefore, to teach from a Christian perspective —
indeed, if we wish to honor the integrity of the academy and the integrity of the Christian tradition, and to honor them both simultaneously — then we must take upon ourselves the paradoxical vision
that stands at the heart of the Christian gospel. For when we embrace that vision, we equip ourselves to do a variety of things in our
classrooms. We equip ourselves, for example, to honor competing
perspectives simultaneously, for one who is comfortable with paradox can be comfortable with competing points of view. If we are
comfortable with paradox, we no longer feel compelled to resolve a
dilemma, to foreclose on a student's question, to eliminate ambiguity, to transform all shades of gray into black or white, or to tie up
every loose end before the class concludes. Again, if we are comfortable with paradox, we can be comfortable with creativity and imagination on the part of our students, even when their creativity forces
us to occupy unfamiliar ground.

In a word, the paradox of the Christian gospel offers an incredibly strong foundation for a classroom that is vibrant, engaged, and
open to new ideas. This is true not simply because the Christian gospel comes to us in the form of a paradox. It is true especially because
the content of that paradox is so incredible: "though we are misera-
ble sinners, we are justified by grace through faith."

For many years, I have quite self-consciously sought to structure
my teaching on the kind of paradoxical vision I have just described. I
make it a point never to preach to my students. But I also make it a
point to let them know, somewhere along the way, that if they find
my classes stimulating and provocative, they must credit the Christian faith, for the Christian faith has given me not only the courage
to teach, but also the courage to take upon myself the contradictions
and the ambiguities that teaching inevitably entails.

Finally, since we have explored in the previous chapter a variety
of theological models for Christian higher education, readers might
legitimately wonder which of these models most informs my own
pedagogical practices. I am convinced that each of the models we re-

viewed in the previous chapter offers enormous resources for those who seek to teach from a Christian perspective. Still, some readers may find it helpful if they can see how I have moved from particular faith perspectives to particular pedagogical practices.

As I indicated in the preface, I am something of a mutt as far as my own faith formation is concerned. I was raised in the Churches of Christ, where I still find my spiritual home. I have been a part of that tradition for so many years that I probably am not completely aware of all the ways it has shaped the way that I think. Yet, some of the debts I owe to the Churches of Christ seem clear. As a denomination with deep roots in the Reformed tradition, it has taught me to acknowledge the sovereignty of God, to trust in Christ for salvation from sin, and to value Scripture. But there is far more than that. For example, in my experience, Churches of Christ have always argued that Scripture must be the final court of appeal for every theological question. In this way, Churches of Christ taught me the virtues of a free and impartial search for truth in religious matters, a perspective that I find enormously supportive for my work in the academy. And the anti-creedal tradition of Churches of Christ has taught me to question all human understandings and all human formulations of the Christian gospel.

Other scholars who do not belong to Churches of Christ but who are nonetheless familiar with that tradition have discerned other points of influence. After reading this book in an early draft, Professor Douglas Jacobsen of Messiah College wrote that he was impressed by the ways in which this essay reflects the values of the Churches of Christ. "What I mean by that," he wrote, "is the mix of enlightenment values, biblicism, self-transcending faith and overall optimism."[1]

Still, as indicated in the preface, there are two other Christian traditions that have profoundly shaped my values and, as a result, the way I teach in the classroom. Martin Luther helped me under-

1. Letter from Douglas Jacobsen to Richard Hughes, December 14, 1999.

What Might It Mean to Teach from a Christian Perspective? 🔊

stand, in ways I had never understood before, the good news that we are justified by grace through faith. In this way, Luther helped me to take upon myself the paradox of the Christian gospel and to embrace both the sovereign grace of God and the ambiguity of the human situation. At the same time, the Anabaptist tradition has helped me to see that the paradox of the Christian gospel must penetrate the very core of our lives as we seek to live out the meaning of "the Upside-Down Kingdom." These perspectives inform my teaching at practically every level.

I want now to turn to the hard question of what it might mean to teach from a Christian perspective. In the material that follows, I will not attempt to identify at every point the ways in which various Christian traditions have shaped my teaching. Yet, in the light of what I have just said, I suspect those influences will be obvious to most discerning readers.

Wonder as an Act of Christian Teaching

The beloved author Madeleine L'Engle rejects the label "Christian writer" as a description of herself and her work. She once wrote,

> Why is it that I, who have spent my life writing, struggling to be a better artist, and struggling also to be a better Christian, should feel rebellious when I am called *a Christian artist?* Why should I feel reluctant to think or write about Christian creativity?[2]

And yet, she is surely one of the most extraordinary Christian writers of our time.

How can this be?

2. Madeleine L'Engle, *Walking on Water: Reflections on Faith and Art* (Wheaton, Ill.: Harold Shaw Publishers, 1980), p. 13.

There are two answers to this question, I think. The first answer emerges when L'Engle recalls her response to a college senior who had asked for help on becoming "a Christian writer." L'Engle told her that "if she is truly and deeply a Christian, what she writes is going to be Christian, whether she mentions Jesus or not. And if she is not, in the most profound sense, Christian, then what she writes is not going to be Christian, no matter how many times she invokes the name of the Lord."[3]

The second answer emerges when we ask about the nature of L'Engle's work. She never sets out to write explicitly Christian books, filled with "Christian answers." Books written with that objective in mind, L'Engle contends, can easily substitute dogmatism for profundity and sentimentality for depth. Even worse, these kinds of books often straitjacket the reader's imagination and leave him or her with little room for individual, creative reflection.[4]

Instead, L'Engle fills her books with wonder. She raises questions and reflects on their meaning. She sends our imaginations spinning into galaxies of reflective thought. She stimulates our creativity and asks us to ponder the meaning of life and the meaning of God. Granted, she does all this within the context of Christian faith. But her work is never didactic.

Her work is never didactic, I would submit, because she consistently writes about the God whose face is the face of mystery, and who therefore shatters the nice, tidy answers that we often like to give. In the presence of such a God, we are forced to wonder, to imagine, and to question yesterday's answers — those answers that seemed so clear at the time.

Paradoxically, then, this woman, who shuns the label "Christian writer," turns out to be a Christian writer of the highest order, for her work embodies the meaning of the Christian paradox at the very

3. L'Engle, *Walking on Water*, pp. 121-22.

4. My wife, Jan, heard Madeleine L'Engle make these comments in a presentation at Evangel College in Springfield, Missouri, probably in 1978 or 1979.

deepest levels. If we could move from writing to teaching, that paradox might look something like this: Cursed is the student of that teacher who deals in finite answers and dogmatic formulations, for that student will discover soon enough how little that teacher really has to say. But blessed is the student of that teacher who embraces wonder and imagination, for that student will soon discover that there is knowing in the midst of not-knowing, and answers in the midst of questions. For when we practice the art of wonder, we begin to discern the God who is both Mystery and Truth and who comes to us in our weakness, not in our strength.

Over the years, therefore, Madeleine L'Engle's work as a "Christian writer" has become a model for my work as a "Christian teacher." It is not my job to present my students with pre-digested answers, but it is my job to inspire wonder, to awaken imagination, to stimulate creativity, and to provide an atmosphere that supports them as, together, we ask questions about meaning and good and evil, about God and life and death.

Even though I teach in a Christian university, I embrace this approach because the immediate context for my work is the academy, not the church. This means that I must respect the integrity of my students and their freedom to raise their own questions and finally to formulate their own answers. But I embrace this approach for a theological reason as well. I embrace it because I serve a God whose majesty defies description, whose sovereignty shatters human orthodoxies of every kind, and who finally forces me to respond, not with answers, but with wonder, creativity, and imagination. If I seek to evoke this sort of response on the part of my students, then I have embraced one of the noblest forms of teaching in which a Christian can engage.

These are the presuppositions that guide my work in the classroom. At some point, I explain these presuppositions to my students, but it never takes them long to figure out those presuppositions for themselves.

Ultimate Questions:
The Ambiguity of the Human Situation

My first objective in every class I teach is to help my students develop an appreciation for human finitude, for limits, for the ambiguity of the human situation — even for the inevitability of death. I grant you, it is difficult to communicate this perspective to eighteen- and twenty-year-old students, but in my view, this is the starting point both for the Christian faith and for any meaningful academic exploration. After all, if we are to hear the gospel, we must confess our finitude, our limitations, and our shortcomings. And if we are to be serious scholars, we must confess that our understandings are inevitably flawed and incomplete. Indeed, we must confess that we could be wrong. If we begin at this point, with an affirmation of our common finitude, we then refuse to juxtapose Christian faith and the life of the mind as if they were diametrically opposite endeavors. Instead, we begin with the one conviction that Christian faith and serious academic exploration share in common: an affirmation of our limitations as human beings.

Some thirty years ago, Gerald Turner, who now serves as the president of Southern Methodist University, was one of my colleagues on the faculty of Pepperdine University. One day, Gerald said to me, "Hughes, it's obvious to me that you have one objective in all your classes." "What's that?" I asked. Gerald looked me straight in the eye and said, half facetiously but also, I thought, half seriously, "You want to convince your students that they're going to die." I've thought about that comment many times over the years, and I've concluded that in many ways, Gerald was right. At the very least, I want my students to be acutely aware of their own limitations — and of *my* limitations. In that way, we know — I and they — that we have much to learn, and we can begin our journey together.

Helping students to come to terms with their finitude, however, is hardly a one-time affair. As human beings, we tend to forget our finitude, to lose sight of our frailties and our limitations in a sea of pretensions that we are something we are not. I remember well a conversation I once had with a UCLA student as we flew five miles above the earth, each of us heading for destinations somewhere in Southern California. She asked me what I did for a living, and I told her I taught religion at Pepperdine. She followed with a series of very perceptive questions. She wanted to know about my presuppositions. I told her that I was convinced of my own limits and that it was important to me to share that perspective with my students. She squared her jaw and said in almost defiant tones, "I don't like limits." Of course, no one does. But to reject the reality of limits is to reject the reality of being human.

This is why I have found so compelling a short story by Garrison Keillor that he calls simply, "Exiles." There, Keillor tells about Larry Sorenson,

> who was saved twelve times in the Lutheran church, an all-time record. Between 1953 and 1961, he threw himself weeping and contrite on God's throne of grace on twelve separate occasions — and this in a Lutheran church that wasn't evangelical. . . . This is the Lutheran church, not a bunch of hillbillies — these are Scandinavians, and they repent in the same way that they sin: discreetly, tastefully, at the proper time, and bring a Jell-O salad for afterward. Larry Sorenson came forward weeping buckets and crumpled up at the communion rail, to the amazement of the minister, who had delivered a dry sermon about stewardship, and who now had to put his arm around this limp, soggy individual and pray with him and see if he had a ride home. *Twelve times.* . . . Granted, we're born in original sin and are worthless and vile, but twelve conversions is too many. God didn't mean us to feel guilty all our lives. There comes a point when you should dry your tears and join the building committee and start grappling with the problems of the church furnace and the church roof

and make church coffee and be of use, but Larry kept on repenting and repenting.[5]

At some point in our lives, most of us dry our tears and join the building committee and forget to repent because we want to deny our limits. This is why, if we intend for our teaching to be rooted in a Christian frame of reference, we must remind ourselves and our students over and over again of the ambiguity of the human situation.

Asking Ultimate Questions

I have sought to accomplish this over the years in virtually all my religion courses by raising at the beginning of each course the very simple question, "What is religion?" I have found Paul Tillich's answer to that question especially meaningful, and I almost always share Tillich's perspectives with my students. From Christianity to Buddhism, from Judaism to Islam, religions — Tillich argues — always seek to provide answers to our ultimate questions. That is the principal task of religion.

But what are those "ultimate questions"? Tillich argues that there is a fundamental difference between important questions and ultimate questions. Whether a student graduates on time is an important question. Whether the publisher accepts that book manuscript that I've been working on for the past fifteen years is an important question. Whether the bank forecloses on my house is an important question. But none of these are ultimate questions.

Ultimate questions for Tillich always focus on matters of life and death. There are three of those questions, Tillich argues, and only three. One doesn't learn to ask these questions by reading the Bible

5. Garrison Keillor, "Exiles," in Paula J. Carlson and Peter S. Hawkins, eds., *Listening for God: Contemporary Literature and the Life of Faith*, vol. 1 (Minneapolis: Augsburg Fortress, 1994), p. 120.

or any other religious book. One learns to ask these questions because one is human. The truth is, we cannot avoid raising these questions because they inevitably well up within us from the depths of our finitude, our brokenness, and our estrangement.

The first of these three questions asks simply, "How can I cope with the inevitability of death?" While that may seem like a terribly remote question for an eighteen-year-old kid, Tillich reminds us that each of us has to face a relative form of this question when we encounter on a daily basis the reality of fate. Why am I blonde? Why am I bald? Why am I tall? Why am I short? Why am a I smart in certain areas, but not so smart in others? Why do good things happen to bad people? Why do bad things happen to good people? These are the multiple faces of fate, but they all share one thing in common: they rob us of our freedom and our autonomy.

When I was a kid growing up in West Texas, I loved basketball. Fortunately for me, I was five feet, nine and one-half inches tall by the time I was thirteen years old. I towered over all my friends, including my teammates on the junior high school basketball team. I knew I was destined for a great career in the NBA. There was no doubt about that. But I hadn't counted on the fact that I had already reached the limit of my growth. Moreover, that inevitable "awkward phase" soon set in, and before long I realized that not only would I never play in the NBA; I would never even play in high school.

Fate in this case was the genetic determination that I would be short, not tall; and awkward, not graceful and coordinated. And when those determinations played themselves out, they robbed me of my autonomy, took away my freedom, and assaulted my pretensions with the reality that I, too, had limits and was only human, after all.

Of course, the various faces of fate are *relative* because we can usually find ways to roll with the punches and cope. If I can't play professional basketball, for example, then perhaps I could be a professor. But there is one dimension of fate that is not relative, but absolute. Here, one does not roll with the punches or find new doors to walk through when other doors close. This dimension of fate is final. It comes to us all. We call it death.

So how can I triumph over fate and death? This is the first of the questions to which all religions respond.

In addition to the question about fate and death, Tillich identifies two additional ultimate questions, each of them ultimate precisely because they, too, speak to matters of life and death. The second question is the question of guilt and condemnation and essentially asks, "Am I an acceptable human being?" The third question asks, "Is there any meaning in life, and if there is, what is it?"

Tillich argues persuasively that in order to remain alive, every human being must answer both of these questions with some degree of affirmation. A sense of self-esteem and a sense of personal meaning are as essential as food, sleep, and water to the continuity of human life. A person who asks, "Am I an acceptable human being?" and can hear only the negative echoes of unrelenting judgment — that person, without help, surely cannot live long. And the person who asks, "What is the meaning in my life?" and can hear in response to that question only the words, "There is no meaning. Life is absurd" — that person, without help, can live in despair only so long, and if the conviction that life is absurd assumes the form of finality with no hope, no ray of light, and no possible sense of meaning whatsoever, we should not be surprised if and when that person finally succumbs to the temptation to take his or her own life.

These, then, are the ultimate questions: the question of fate and death, the question of guilt and condemnation, and the question of emptiness and meaninglessness. These questions, if we pay them serious regard, always reveal to us the extent of our limitations and the depth of our finitude and alienation.

Some years ago, when I taught at a Christian university in Texas, I asked a class to think about the question of emptiness and meaninglessness. I wanted them to see that meaning is an indispensable ingredient for the maintenance of human life. And so I asked, "If a person asks about the meaning of his or her life, and the answer comes back, 'There is no meaning,' where is that person likely to be in very short order?" I had in mind the grave. But the students were slow to get the point, and so they thought, and they thought. A minute went by, perhaps two minutes, and then, finally, one student raised his hand and in all seriousness blurted out, "The University of Texas?" Ah, that wonderful distinction between Christian and public higher education!

So What Have We Achieved?

I want us now to think about what we achieve when we get our students to think about fate and death and emptiness and meaninglessness and guilt and condemnation in these ways.

First, if we can prompt our students to embrace the ambiguity of the human situation, we may also prompt them to give serious consideration to the reality of God. After all, if a student cannot come to terms with the ambiguity of human life and with his or her own personal frailties and limitations, if that student still labors under the illusion — as many of our students do — that one can transcend limitations and achieve infinite fame, infinite wealth, and infinite power, then that student is not likely to respond to any religious tradition including the Christian faith. And so, if I have any hope that my students might take the Christian message seriously, it becomes my task — my very first task — to awaken them to their humanness, with all that that entails. This, it seems to me, is the indispensable starting point for any meaningful education in the Christian genre.

Second, by asking our students to take seriously their own finitude — and the finitude of others — we free them for a healthy skepticism, not only of their own self-sufficiency, but also of the presumed self-sufficiency of others. We free them to question the wisdom of all human authorities, including the wisdom they may learn from us. And we free them to doubt the finality of all human solutions, especially those that masquerade under the label "final solutions."

Third, by asking our students to take seriously their own finitude, we prepare them to take seriously the finitude of others, to appreciate the common bond that ties them to all other human beings, and to reach out with compassionate sensitivity to those who suffer from disease, misfortune, oppression, and need.

And fourth, by focusing our attention on ultimate questions, not on religious answers, we preserve our students' integrity and guarantee their freedom to make religious discoveries for themselves.

I do not mean to suggest that in order to accomplish these objectives, you should employ Tillich's categories as I do. But I do mean to suggest that getting our students to reflect on the meaning of their finitude, the meaning of their estrangement, and the meaning of their inevitable deaths is absolutely crucial to the task of Christian higher education.

At this point, I find immensely helpful an observation from Professor Mark Schwehn, Dean of Christ College at Valparaiso University. Schwehn perceptively asks,

> Can a liberal democracy continue to be served by a higher education that exalts ideals of freedom, enlightenment, progressive development, problem-solving, and the relief of humankind's estate without commensurate attention to the meaning and significance of the overwhelming facts of human mortality and finitude? Or, to put the matter more bluntly, can higher learning remain credible in [this] century in the face of the facts of the past century, if it continues as a kind of subtle denial of death?[6]

6. Mark Schwehn, "Lutheran Higher Education in the Twenty-First Century," a paper delivered at the "Conference on the Future of Religious Colleges," Harvard University, October 7, 2000.

Morrie Schwartz, the Brandeis sociologist who came to terms with the meaning of life in the very throes of death, and whose wise observations were immortalized in the best-selling book *Tuesdays with Morrie,* offered this piece of advice: "Learn how to die, and you learn how to live."[7] If we wish to help our students learn to live their lives in meaningful ways — and surely this must be a fundamental objective of Christian higher education — then we must encourage our students to embrace their finitude and to grapple forthrightly with the ultimate questions of human existence.

And yet, to this point, we have done only half of what needs to be done in the context of Christian higher education. To this point, we have only raised questions. How is it possible, then, to correlate those questions with distinctly Christian answers while at the same time maintaining an atmosphere conducive to freedom, discovery, and creativity?

Christian Answers:
The Values of the Upside-Down Kingdom

In order to make the second half of our journey, we must explore the meaning of the kingdom of God. Mary, the mother of Jesus, gives us our very first insight into the nature of that kingdom when she "rejoices in God my Savior,"

> for he has been mindful
>   of the humble state of his servant. . . .
> He has performed mighty deeds with his arm;
>   he has scattered those who are proud in their
>   inmost thoughts.
> He has brought down rulers from their thrones
>   but has lifted up the humble.

7. Mitch Albom, *Tuesdays with Morrie* (New York: Doubleday, 1997), p. 83.

He has filled the hungry with good things
  but has sent the rich away empty.   (Luke 1:47-48, 51-53)

This statement from Mary suggests that the kingdom of God would be no ordinary kingdom embracing traditional values, but instead would turn traditional values upside down. Instead of exalting the rich at the expense of the poor, this kingdom would exalt the poor at the expense of the rich. Instead of exalting the powerful at the expense of the powerless, this kingdom would bring down those who exalt themselves and raise the humble to a high degree.

If we are Christians, how might this vision of the kingdom of God shape our teaching? I submit that if our teaching is in sync with the values of the kingdom of God, we will find ways to communicate those values to our students. This means that our teaching will often turn out to be radical, even dangerous since, in effect, we will serve as ambassadors for a kingdom that turns traditional values on their heads.

Choosing What to Teach

The process of communicating kingdom values to our students rests on several foundations. We laid the first of these foundations when we encouraged our students to reflect on the meaning of finitude, alienation, and death. After all, a student who has never seriously considered these fundamental dimensions of human life is hardly prepared to understand, much less to embrace, the radical values of the kingdom of God.

The second step in communicating kingdom values to our students begins when we choose *what* we will teach. Traditional values demand that we teach facts, because facts by themselves are tame and never disrupt the status quo. On the other hand, kingdom values demand that we explore the *meaning* of the facts and that we inquire whether those facts reflect justice and peace and service to the neighbor or whether those facts reflect oppression and exploitation.

Let me give you an example. An American political scientist and historian named Howard Zinn wrote in a small book called *Failure to Quit* the following poignant lines.

> In May 1976, the *New York Times* published a series of articles lamenting the ignorance of American students about their own history. The *Times* was pained. Four leading historians whom it consulted were also pained. It seemed students did not know that James Polk was president during the Mexican War, that James Madison was president during the War of 1812, that the Homestead Act was passed earlier than Civil Service reform, or that the Constitution authorizes Congress to regulate interstate commerce but says nothing about the cabinet.
>
> We might wonder if the *Times,* or its historian-consultants, learned anything from the history of this century. It has been a century of atrocities: the death camps of Hitler, the slave camps of Stalin, the devastation of Southeast Asia by the United States. All of these were done by powerful leaders and obedient populations in countries that had achieved high levels of literacy and education. . . .
>
> Surely, how "smart" a person is on history tests like this one devised by the *Times* . . . tells you nothing about whether that person is decent or indecent, violent or peaceful, whether that person will resist evil by becoming a consultant to warmakers, will become a Pastor Niemoller (a German who resisted the Nazis) or an Albert Speer (who worked for them), a Lieutenant Calley (who killed children at My Lai) or a Flight Officer Thompson (who tried to save them).[8]

8. Howard Zinn, *Failure to Quit* (Monroe, Maine: Common Courage Press, 1993), pp. 40-41.

The truth is, Howard Zinn is not a Christian. And yet, I have found his passion for peace and justice fundamentally compatible with the kingdom vision I wish to share with my students. I well remember that day some twenty-five years ago when I wandered into a bookstore in Springfield, Missouri, and found on its shelves Zinn's marvelous book entitled *A People's History of the United States*. I perused this book and quickly discovered that it was like no American history text I had ever seen. If most histories of the United States told their stories from the perspective of presidents, generals, entrepreneurs, and power-brokers, Zinn told the story from the perspective of the little people: blacks, poor whites, Native Americans, women, and common laborers. In my judgment, Zinn's book is profoundly Christian in its orientation, not because the book is written by a Christian since, of course, it is not. Rather, it is profoundly Christian because it embraces the same "upside-down" values that we have been taught by the Christian faith.

It is worth listening to Zinn as he describes his rationale for this approach.

> When I taught American history, I ignored the canon of the traditional textbooks, in which the heroic figures were mostly presidents, generals, and industrialists. In those texts, wars were treated as problems in military strategy and not in morality; Christopher Columbus and Andrew Jackson and Theodore Roosevelt were treated as heroes in the march of democracy, with not a word from the objects of their violence.
>
> I suggested that we approach Columbus and Jackson from the perspective of their victims, that we look at the magnificent feat of the transcontinental railroad from the viewpoint of the Irish and Chinese laborers who, in building it, died by the thousands.[9]

9. Zinn, *Failure to Quit*, pp. 90-91.

Based on this perspective, I decided some years ago that I would build units into my courses that would force my students to take seriously the poor, the oppressed, and people who were objects of discrimination. Beyond this, I wanted to motivate my students to become agents for peace and justice in the world.

Several years ago, I taught a freshman seminar entitled "Religion and Race in America." I wanted my students to gain some understanding of the history and the faith of African Americans in the United States. We read wonderful books like *The Narrative of Frederick Douglass,* Richard Wright's *Black Boy,* Eldridge Cleaver's *Soul on Ice,* and Martin Luther King's *Why We Can't Wait.* In addition, during the course of that semester I showed all fourteen films in the "Eyes on the Prize" series that documents so beautifully the Civil Rights Movement in the United States. There were many days when a film reached its conclusion, only to find me and the students sitting in our seats, looking at one another, literally stunned into silence. What could we say?

By the close of the semester, one student announced that she had been so moved by what she had learned in this course that she had determined to become a civil rights attorney and to fight for the rights of the oppressed. That was in her freshman year. Four years later, she graduated with well over a 3.8 GPA. A few months before her commencement, she came by my office with a large stack of applications to some of the best law schools in the country: Harvard, Yale, Berkeley, Georgetown, UCLA, and others. She wanted me to write a series of recommendations. "Are you still determined to become a civil rights attorney?" I asked. She assured me that she was, though I was happy to write the recommendations regardless of her response to that question.

I know that my course was not the only course that helped shape the thinking and commitments of this student. Nonetheless, her decision was for me a triumph, and as far as I was concerned, it was a triumph for Christian higher education.

I submit that when we focus our students' attention on the poor, the marginalized, and the oppressed, we accomplish a number of objectives that must be fundamental to the mission of any Christian institution of higher learning. First, we encourage our students to take seriously the ambiguity of the human situation, for nothing can be more ambiguous than human life that is marginalized. Second, by teaching in this way, we allow our students to see the very face of God, for according to Scripture, God wears the face of the poor and has taken upon himself the ambiguity of the human situation. Third, by teaching in this way, we create a marvelous opportunity to encourage our students to serve as agents of peace and justice and reconciliation.

Teaching with Passion

And yet, our students may see none of these points unless we take a third step which I want to call teaching with passion. By invoking the word "passion," I do not mean that we should teach with artificial enthusiasm, or that we should somehow serve as academic cheerleaders who seek to create in our classrooms excitement for excitement's sake. No, when I use the word "passion," I mean to suggest that we must teach in ways that stimulate our students to exercise their God-given imagination and creativity and free them to wonder, to search, and explore.

Beyond this, there is another dimension of passionate teaching. For we must help our students to realize their human capacity not only to think but also to feel. We must grieve with those who grieve and rejoice with those who rejoice. If we care about what we communicate to our students, then we cannot afford to teach as if what we share with them finally makes no difference. Passionate teaching means that we allow what we teach to awaken not only our minds, but also our *feelings* and our *emotions*.

Passionate teaching also means that while we may very well employ multi-media technology to get across a given lesson, we never allow technology to displace the human interaction that can occur between ourselves and our students. Indeed, passionate teaching means that we choose modes of discourse that are fundamentally humane, words that engage instead of stifle the imagination. Passionate teaching means that we never substitute data for ideas. And perhaps most important, passionate teaching means that we never substitute the language of authoritarian discourse for genuine dialogue with other visions, other cultures, and other ideas.

In her Nobel Lecture delivered in Stockholm in 1993, Toni Morrison explains that those who seek to stifle imagination and suppress human creativity must first kill the language. "A dead language," she writes,

> is not only one no longer spoken or written, it is unyielding language content to admire its own paralysis. Like statist language, censored and censoring. Ruthless in its policing duties, it has no desire or purpose other than to maintain the free range of its own narcotic narcissism, its own exclusivity and dominance. . . . It actively thwarts the intellect, stalls conscience, suppresses human potential. Unreceptive to interrogation, it cannot form or tolerate new ideas, shape other thoughts, tell another story, fill baffling silences. . . .
>
> The systematic looting of language can be recognized by the tendency of its users to forego its nuanced, complex, midwifery properties, replacing them with menace and subjugation. Oppressive language does more than represent violence; it is violence; does more than represent the limits of knowledge; it limits knowledge. Whether it is obscuring state language or the faux language of mindless media; whether it is the proud but calcified language of the academy or the commodity-driven language of science; whether it is the malign language of law-without-ethics, or language designed for the estrangement of minorities, hiding its racist plunder in its literary cheek — it must be rejected, altered and exposed. It is

the language that drinks blood, laps vulnerabilities, tucks its fascist boots under crinolines of respectability and patriotism as it moves relentlessly toward the bottom line and the bottomed-out mind. Sexist language, racist language, theistic language — all are typical of the policing languages of mastery, and cannot, do not, permit new knowledge or encourage the mutual exchange of ideas.[10]

The fact that Morrison classes theistic language with sexist language and racist language is important, for we must acknowledge that despots have employed theistic language in all cultures and all periods of human history to suppress imagination, to stifle creativity, and to kill the human spirit. Indeed, theistic language used in this way is language void of passion.

But theistic language used in its biblical sense is liberating language and humanizing language not only because God is God, but also because theistic language in its biblical sense is passionate language.

The noted Old Testament scholar Walter Brueggemann argues that tyrants in every age have sought to suppress the human spirit by robbing language of its power to inquire, by reducing language to data and facts and sound bites and statistics, by promoting a language that cannot convey grief or joy or love or passion in any form. This is the language of despots, of totalitarian regimes, or to use Brueggemann's words, this is the language of "the royal consciousness" or "the imperial reality."

This is precisely why Brueggemann argues that passion is so central to the discourse of the Old Testament prophets. Brueggemann writes,

I believe that the possibility of passion is a primary prophetic agenda and that it is precisely what the royal consciousness

10. Toni Morrison, *The Nobel Lecture in Literature, 1993* (New York: Alfred A. Knopf, 1994), pp. 13-17.

means to eradicate. Passion as the capacity and readiness to care, to suffer, to die, and to feel is the enemy of imperial reality. Imperial economics is designed to keep people satiated so that they do not notice. Its politics is intended to block out the cries of the denied ones. Its religion is to be an opiate so that no one discerns misery alive in the heart of God. Pharaoh, the passive king in the block universe, in the land without revolution or change or history or promise or hope, is the model king for a world that never changes from generation to generation.[11]

On the other hand, the Hebrew prophets proclaim a God who acts, who breaks into human history, who brings promise and hope, who offers transformation and redemption.

This is precisely why those of us who believe in this God-Who-Acts must celebrate this God with passionate expectation. This is why it makes no sense for teachers in Christian institutions to teach as if we have no hope, to teach in uncreative ways, or to teach in ways that never evoke imagination on the part of our students. This is why it makes no sense for teachers in Christian institutions to use words and strategies that betray an allegiance to the static world of Pharaoh instead of an allegiance to the God-Who-Acts. Put another way, the fact that we serve a God who creates and redeems, who liberates and transforms — the fact that we serve this God is precisely why we must teach with hope. And when we teach with hope, we will inescapably teach with imagination, with creativity, with passion.

11. Walter Brueggemann, *The Prophetic Imagination* (Minneapolis: Fortress Press, 1978), p. 41.

Conclusions

I want to conclude by telling a story that sums up much that I have tried to say in this chapter.

Eldridge Cleaver, Minister of Information for the Black Panther Party during the 1960s, wrote from his prison cell a testament of the times which he called *Soul on Ice*. There, Cleaver told of a marvelous teacher named Chris Lovdjieff who taught at San Quentin Prison on a regular basis.[12] Cleaver called Lovdjieff, simply, "The Christ." Whether Lovdjieff was Christian or not, I do not know. But his teaching embodies the characteristics that I have discussed in this essay.

Cleaver tells us that Lovdjieff was so incredibly effective that

> the officials would sometimes have to send a guard to his class to make him stop teaching, so the inmates could be locked up for the night. He was horror-stricken that they could make such a demand of him. Reluctantly, he'd sit down heavily in his seat, burdened by defeat, and tell us to go to our cells. Part of the power we gave him was that we would never leave his class unless he himself dismissed us. If a guard came and told us to leave, he got only cold stares; we would not move until Lovdjieff gave the word.

Why were these prisoners so devoted to Lovdjieff? Why did they hang on his every word? And why did Cleaver call him "The Christ"?

First, like any great teacher, Lovdjieff resisted orthodoxies of every kind, and he resisted those orthodoxies precisely because he had come to terms with the ambiguities of the human situation. Cleaver recalled,

> I got the impression that the carnage of World War II, particularly the scientific, systematic approach to genocide of the

12. Eldridge Cleaver, *Soul on Ice* (New York: Dell, 1968), pp. 31-39.

What Might It Mean to Teach from a Christian Perspective? ⟡

Nazi regime, had been a traumatic experience from which it was impossible for him to recover. It was as if he had seen or experienced something which had changed him forever, sickened his soul, overwhelmed him with sympathy and love for all mankind. He hated all restraints upon the human mind, the human spirit, all blind believing, all dogmatic assertions. He questioned everything.

Second, Lovdjieff, whether Christian or not, nonetheless embodied the principles of the Upside-Down Kingdom. As Cleaver explains, "Lovdjieff's central quality seemed to be pain, suffering, and a peculiar strength based on his understanding of his own helplessness, weakness, and need." Perhaps because of this quality, Lovdjieff

was drawn to those students who seemed most impossible to teach — old men who had been illiterate all their lives and set in their ways. Lovdjieff didn't believe that anyone or anything in the universe was "set in its ways." Those students who were intelligent and quickest to learn he seemed reluctant to bother with, almost as if to say, pointing at the illiterates and speaking to the bright ones: "Go away. Leave me. You don't need me. These others do."

And third, Lovdjieff taught with passion.

Once he was lecturing on the ancient Hebrews. He was angry with them for choosing to settle along the trade routes between Egypt and Mesopotamia. He showed how, over the centuries, time and time again, these people had been invaded, slaughtered, driven out, captured, but always to return.

"What is it that keeps pulling them back to this spot!" he exclaimed. He lost his breath. His face crumbled, and he broke down and wept. "Why do they insist on living in the middle of that — that [for once, I thought meanly, The Christ couldn't find a word] that — that — Freeway! . . . That's all it is — look!" He pointed out the trade routes on the map behind his desk, then he sat down and cried uncontrollably for several minutes.

Another time, he brought tape-recorded selections from Thomas Wolfe's *Look Homeward Angel*. The Christ wept all through the tape.

The Christ could weep over a line of poetry, over a single image in a poem, over the beauty of a poem's music, over the fact that man can talk, read, write, walk, reproduce, die, eat, eliminate — over the fact that a chicken can lay an egg.

Given what we know about the nature of the "royal consciousness," it is little wonder that the prison officials finally barred Lovdjieff from teaching at all.

My task as a Christian teacher is to do all that Lovdjieff did, but from my perspective, I must go one step further. I must let my students know that I have chosen *to* teach, that I have chosen *what* to teach, and that I have chosen to teach with passion and concern, not because I am liberal or conservative, not because I subscribe to a particular political orientation, and certainly not because I seek to be politically correct, but rather because of my commitment to the Lord of the Upside-Down Kingdom. That commitment is precisely what enables us to resist sterile orthodoxies, to nurture imagination and creativity on the part of our students, and to encourage the free exchange of ideas. This, in my judgment, is at least part of what it means to teach from a Christian perspective.

CHAPTER SIX

The Questions of Distinctiveness
and Proclamation

IN THE PRECEDING CHAPTERS I HAVE TRIED TO ILLUSTRATE SOME of the ways that Christian faith can sustain Christian scholars as they seek to nurture the life of the mind, as they seek to enlarge their sphere of academic freedom, and as they attempt to enhance the quality of their classroom teaching.

From those who heard some of this material presented orally, or read various selections in manuscript form, the response has been amazingly varied. Some have thought the approach of this text insufficiently confrontational when it comes to the truth claims of the Christian gospel. Thus, after hearing the previous chapter presented orally, one colleague raised the pointed question, "What you have done here is all fine and good, but where's the proclamation?"

On the other hand, some have found the approach of this book far *too* Christian in its orientation. Several times, after presenting portions of this material orally, I encountered the question from Christian scholars at various church-related colleges and universities, "Why go to so much trouble to ground what you do in Christian faith?"

In that context, after he had read this text almost in its entirety, one of my Jewish colleagues at Pepperdine University frankly observed, "You envision teaching and scholarship precisely as I envision teaching and scholarship. You value openness, diversity, and an unrelenting search for truth, just as I do. But why must you go through such theological gymnastics to get where you're going when you and I arrive at the very same place in the end?"

These questions are so penetrating that we dare not ignore them.

How Distinctively "Christian" Must Christian Scholarship Be?

The question from my Jewish colleague is in some respects the most probing of all. Why not just embrace good pedagogical practices and be done with it? Why feel compelled to ground one's teaching and scholarship in Christian faith?

As far as I am concerned, the answer to that question is clear and simple, but also highly personal. I can state it in four short words: I am a Christian. That fact places other scholars under no obligation whatsoever, but it places me under a profound obligation. Indeed, that fact must inevitably lend shape and texture to all that I do. It is simply unthinkable that I should practice my teaching and my scholarship in one corner of my life, and practice my Christian faith in another so that never the twain shall meet. Because I am a committed Christian on the one hand and a committed scholar and teacher on the other, I must find some way to integrate these two core dimensions that define who I am at the most basic levels of my life.

But what of my Jewish colleague's observation that, when all is said and done, he and I come out at precisely the same place? He values diversity; so do I. He values openness; so do I. He values the search for truth; so do I. Since he makes no pretense of grounding his teaching and scholarship in a Christian frame of reference, does not the fact that we share so much common ground constitute a fundamental indictment of the approach I have developed in this text?

To the contrary, I rejoice that he and I share so much in common pedagogically. I rejoice because, from my perspective, his work constitutes scholarship of the very highest sort. And I am grateful that he views my work in the very same light. But I rejoice as well over the fact that I have embraced those canons of scholarship precisely *because* I am a Christian, not *in spite of* that fact.

What I am trying to say is this: I am not concerned that my scholarship and my teaching differ dramatically from what is generally considered sound scholarship and good teaching in the academy at large. But I am concerned that if I am able to reach the highest levels of scholarship and teaching, I do so precisely *because of* my commitment to the Christian faith, not *in spite of* that commitment. Put another way, I am concerned to allow the presuppositions of the Christian faith to provide the underpinnings and the framework for how I envision my work, for how I think about my discipline, for how I structure my arguments, and for how I teach in the classroom. Or put another way still, I want to think "Christianly" about my teaching and about my scholarship. If, in the process of doing so, my work finally resembles that of other academicians — even secular academicians — who are generally regarded as serious scholars and teachers, then I can only rejoice that, at least in some measure, I have successfully integrated my Christian faith with my life's work.

The question, then, is not whether my work consistently embodies distinctively Christian language, themes, or ideas. Indeed, it is conceivable that a work of scholarship adorned with Christian language and Christian themes could be fundamentally anti-Christian at the most basic level possible — the level of first-order presuppositions and commitments. In this context, we must remember the advice that Madeleine L'Engle gave to the student who sought to become a "Christian writer." L'Engle told her that "if she is truly and deeply a Christian, what she writes is going to be Christian, whether she mentions Jesus or not. And if she is not, in the most profound sense, Christian, then what she writes is not going to be Christian, no matter how many times she invokes the name of the Lord."[1]

---

1. Madeleine L'Engle, *Walking on Water: Reflections on Faith and Art* (Wheaton, Ill.: Harold Shaw Publishers, 1980), pp. 121-22.

The truth is, if we wish to succeed at this business of Christian scholarship, we must go far deeper than cosmetic appearances. The real question I must ask is whether my work is grounded in Christian presuppositions, a Christian frame of reference, or — as Reformed thinkers might put it — a Christian worldview. It is appropriate in this context to recall once again the words of Professor Paul Griffiths of the University of Chicago Divinity School. "One is a Christian scholar," Griffiths contends, "if one understands one's work to be based upon and framed by and always in the service of one's identity as a Christian."

Let me offer just one example. I suspect that few readers would regard Parker Palmer's magnificent book, *The Courage to Teach*, as a distinctively Christian text. The book nowhere mentions Jesus, the Trinity, or even God, for that matter, and it nowhere identifies itself as a Christian text or a text written in the service of the Christian tradition. Outside of a short section slightly more than three pages long on "Knowing and the Sacred," there is little about this book that calls our attention in any sort of direct or forthright way to explicitly religious issues. Christian "window dressing" is simply not a part of this text. What is more, this book has drawn praise since its publication in 1998 from Christian educators, but also from "secular" educators who have little or no interest in Christian themes, Christian scholarship, or Christian education.

Yet, in my judgment, *The Courage to Teach* is a profoundly Christian book and, as far as I can tell, quite deliberately so. The truth is, *The Courage to Teach* is grounded at almost every step of the way in Palmer's Quaker heritage.[2] This fact must be obvious to any

2. Palmer forthrightly acknowledges the Quaker tradition as the root of his creative thinking about education in two documents: " 'Meeting for Learning' Revisited: Trailing Quaker Crumbs Through the Wilderness of Higher Education," a presentation to the Friends Council on Education and the Friends Association of Higher Education, held at Earlham College, May 2000; and "Meeting for Learning: Education in a Quaker Context," a pamphlet published by the Friends Council on Education. While Palmer does not dwell on the Quaker roots of his thought in *The*

reader of Palmer's text who also knows something about the Quaker tradition.

For 350 years, Quakers have prized the "Inner Light" or "That of God" that resides in all men and women, and the reality of the "Inner Light" has determined the shape of the Quaker "meeting." If most Christians — Catholics and Protestants alike — have structured their meetings around the authority of the cleric and therefore sit in pews, staring at the backs of each other's heads, Quakers have moved in a very different direction. Because they believe so strongly in "That of God" that indwells every human being, Quakers have most often structured their meetings in a circle. They gather in that circle, not to hear a preacher or some other authority figure, but rather to hear one another as each of them interprets for the meeting the promptings of the "Light Within."

From the beginning, the Quaker meeting was egalitarian. George Foxe, the Quaker founder, argued that since God gave the gift of the "Inner Light" to all human beings, the voices of all should be accorded equal value. It made no difference whether one was rich or poor, black or white, male or female. All possessed "That of God Within," and for that reason, each person had something of value to contribute to the meeting.

Parker Palmer's *The Courage to Teach*, therefore, introduces us to concepts like "the teacher within," the voice of identity and integrity that indwells both teacher and student. When Palmer begins to explore the ways in which we might structure our classrooms, he therefore rejects — not surprisingly — the "teacher-centered" model on the grounds that it tends toward absolutistic authoritarianism. But he also rejects the popular "student-centered" model on the grounds that it tends toward relativism. Instead, Palmer advo-

---

Courage to Teach, that book does offer hints of that influence as, for example, when he explores the use of the "clearness committee" to help faculty become better teachers. Parker Palmer, *The Courage to Teach* (San Francisco: Jossey-Bass, 1998), pp. 151-52.

§   *The Vocation of the Christian Scholar*

cates a "subject-centered" model that transcends both teacher and students. He argues for a "community of truth" or a "circle of seekers" in which students and teacher alike gather around the subject, described here as a "great thing." "By *great things*," Palmer writes, "I mean the subjects around which the circle of seekers has always gathered — not the disciplines that study these subjects, not the texts that talk about them, not the theories that explain them, but the things themselves."[3]

True to his Quaker heritage, Palmer argues that the voice of every person in the "circle of seekers" must be heard. Accordingly, he writes,

- We invite *diversity* into our community not because it is politically correct but because diverse viewpoints are demanded by the manifold mysteries of great things.
- We embrace *ambiguity* not because we are confused or indecisive but because we understand the inadequacy of our concepts to embrace the vastness of great things.
- We welcome *creative conflict* not because we are angry or hostile but because conflict is required to correct our biases and prejudices about the nature of great things.[4]

Parker Palmer has written a book that appears to be — and, in fact, in many ways is — a secular text for a secular audience on a secular topic: the improvement of classroom teaching. At the same time, this text draws so profoundly on the riches of the Quaker tradition that I am forced to regard it as one of the finest examples of Christian scholarship that I have encountered. I regard this book in this way, not because it promotes itself as a Christian text since most certainly it does not, but rather because its secular content draws strength and power from a Christian vision of reality.

3. Palmer, *The Courage to Teach*, p. 107.
4. Palmer, *The Courage to Teach*, p. 107.

The Question of "Proclamation"

From all that I have written both in this and previous chapters, it must be clear that while I seek to ground my teaching and my scholarship in a Christian frame of reference, I also hope that my academic work will exhibit the very highest standards of good scholarship. At this point, someone might well raise the question, "In your zeal to embrace the canons of good scholarship, have you not slighted the Christian faith? Or to put the question another way, have you not conformed the Christian faith to the canons of good scholarship instead of conforming your scholarship to the standards of the Christian faith?"

In some ways, the colleague who asked the question about proclamation, mentioned earlier in this chapter, anticipated this very issue. At the very least, he would have been far more pleased had I made room for the forthright proclamation of the gospel of Jesus Christ in the context of our classroom teaching, if not in the context of our written scholarship.

To this expectation, I can only state my conviction that it is a very great honor to proclaim the gospel of Jesus Christ and to do so on a regular basis. But if I had wished to make that honor a fundamental dimension of my vocation, I should have become a preacher, not a teacher.

Having said that, we must also admit that when we focus classroom discussions on ultimate questions of purpose and meaning — as indeed we should — have we not guided our students into the very starting point for the Christian gospel? And when we focus our students' attention on the poor, the marginalized, and the oppressed, or when we encourage our students to serve as agents of peace, justice, and reconciliation, have we not thereby engaged in the very first order of Christian proclamation?

But there is more, for Parker Palmer also reminds us that we inevitably "teach who we are."[5] The fact that we "teach who we are"

---

5. Palmer, *The Courage to Teach*, pp. 1-7.

does not provide us with an excuse for propagandizing in the classroom. But it does free each of us, in the context of our work as teachers, to take seriously our core identity as human beings. In my case, and in the case of countless other Christian scholars and teachers, the Christian faith has defined that identity and therefore helps determine what we teach, how we teach, and why.

While I avoid propagandizing in the classroom, I am quick to let my students know that I am a Christian. I neither dwell on that fact nor make an issue of it. But once I have made that point, many of my students are quick to discern *why* I wish to explore with them the questions of fate and death, or emptiness and meaninglessness, or guilt and condemnation. And they are equally quick to discern *why* I encourage them to take seriously the marginalized and the dispossessed. Once the students know *who I am* and *where my deepest commitments lie,* they have a context for understanding everything that goes on in my classroom.

This approach may not satisfy my friend who asked, "But where's the proclamation?" The fact is, some students will find in this approach no proclamation at all. But students with eyes to see and ears to hear may well discern in this approach a kind of proclamation that transforms their own thinking and commitments in radical and far-reaching ways.

Still and all, I have made no attempt in this book to provide a theoretical rationale for making the proclamation of the Christian gospel a fundamental part of our teaching and our scholarship. Instead, I have sought to offer ways in which Christian scholars can embrace the very best pedagogical practices and the highest standards of scholarship and do so *precisely because of* their allegiance to the Christian faith. Put another way, I am not concerned to ask how Christian scholars can legitimately engage in "proclamation." But I am concerned to ask how Christian scholars can employ the Christian gospel as a foundational presupposition for their work. Or, put another way still, I have simply sought in this book to ask how the Christian gospel can sustain the life of the mind.

Christian Faith and the Life of the Mind

But I still have not addressed in any adequate way the question that a Christian scholar, having read this book, might pose directly at me: have I not conformed my understanding of the Christian faith to the canons of good scholarship rather than the other way around?

The truth is, I find myself in the happy position of believing that many of the values that are central to good scholarship and sound teaching are values that also lie at the heart of the Christian faith.

Parker Palmer, for example, argues that the notion of paradox is fundamental to good teaching. Palmer cites Niels Bohr, the Nobel Prize-winning physicist who observed that "the opposite of a true statement is a false statement, but the opposite of a profound truth can be another profound truth." Palmer laments the fact that most teachers — indeed, most Westerners in general — tend to think the world apart into true/false, black/white, good/bad, or sacred/secular, and to isolate profound truths in these and other kinds of air-tight compartments. On the other hand, Palmer suggests that good teachers will hold profound truths in paradoxical tension, even when the pressure is great to think them apart. When we hold profound truths in paradoxical tension, Palmer believes, we and our students can benefit from questions and from insights that would be impossible to discern if we confined ourselves to binary categories.[6]

At the very same time, the notion of paradox stands at the core of the Christian gospel — a point I have made time and again throughout this text. If, therefore, I have embraced the paradox of the Christian gospel in my life and in my thinking, then I am far more capable of embracing the concept of paradox in my teaching and in my scholarship than otherwise might be the case.

Or again, good scholarship takes seriously the reality of human limitations and the ambiguity of the human situation. Good scholars are therefore quick to confess that there is much that we misunder-

6. Palmer, *The Courage to Teach*, pp. 61-87.

The Vocation of the Christian Scholar

stand and much that we simply don't know. This is precisely why scholars *must* embrace the search for truth. But this conviction, so central to good scholarship, is also fundamental to the Christian faith, since Christian faith proclaims that all men and women have fallen woefully short of the glory of the infinite God. If, as a Christian, I take that confession seriously, I am far better prepared to acknowledge my intellectual limitations than might be the case otherwise.

Or again, good scholarship is scholarship in the service of humanity, not scholarship that is content to serve its own agenda. Of all people, Christian scholars should have no trouble embracing this understanding of scholarship since we have been taught to give ourselves for the neighbor just as God in Christ has given himself for us.

And finally, good scholarship is skeptical scholarship. It raises questions and doubts the legitimacy of easy answers. At precisely this point, however, many Christians may find a significant level of tension between scholarship and the Christian faith. After all, does not the Christian faith provide final answers to ultimate questions, answers that must be accepted and embraced?

At one level, that is true. But we must also recall that our ability to comprehend final answers to ultimate questions is meager, indeed. That, too, is a fundamental teaching of biblical faith. For this reason, Christians must embrace doubt as a central dimension of belief. The Spanish philosopher Miguel De Unamuno perhaps put it best when he wrote that "those who believe they believe in God, but without passion in the heart, without anguish of mind, without uncertainty, without doubt, and even at times without despair, believe only in the idea of God, and not in God himself."[7]

It is for this reason that I continue to find central to the task of scholarship the confession made to Jesus by the father of the demon-possessed son: "Lord, I believe; help thou mine unbelief" (Mark 9:24). This is why I have argued in this book that Christian

7. Cited in L'Engle, *Walking on Water*, p. 32.

scholars, of all people, must find ways to affirm and break through the particularities of their faith, and to do so over and over again. This is the paradox that Christian scholars must take upon themselves if they wish to be faithful to the life of the mind and faithful to their Christian convictions, and to honor both sides of this equation simultaneously.

Christian scholars must search diligently for truth and affirm with conviction and affirmation those things that can be affirmed. But they must also allow the wonders and the mysteries of the Christian faith to inspire doubt and, at certain levels, even skepticism. For skepticism and doubt breed questions, and without the questions, there can be no life of the mind.

The Vocation of a Christian College; or, What Makes Church-Related Education Christian?

T HE 1990S WITNESSED A PLETHORA OF BOOKS AND ARTICLES exploring the thesis that the Christian dimension of church-related higher education has been in steady decline from the late nineteenth century until now.[1] That thesis inevitably raises the question of this chapter: "What makes church-related education Christian?" Or, to frame this question in another way, "What is the authentic vocation of a Christian institution of higher learning?"

I want to address this question by posing a two-fold thesis of my own. First, if a church-related college or university aspires to serve as a *Christian* institution, that college or university must ground every aspect of its work in a theological frame of reference.

Pragmatic considerations, so common in merely church-related education, are insufficient to drive enrollment decisions, marketing decisions, curricular decisions, and decisions that bear on student life. To be sure, no institution can escape pragmatic considerations. At the same time, Christian colleges and universities should ground *all* strategic decisions in a shared theological vision. Without that di-

---

1. The work of George Marsden and James Burtchaell is particularly noteworthy in this regard. See George Marsden, *The Soul of the American University: From Protestant Establishment to Established Nonbelief* (Oxford: Oxford University Press, 1994); and James Tunstead Burtchaell, *The Dying of the Light: The Disengagement of Colleges and Universities from Their Christian Churches* (Grand Rapids: Eerdmans, 1998).

mension, a church-related college or university can hardly claim much depth as a Christian institution.

Stanley Hauerwas affirmed in his Gifford Lectures for 2001 that the question for him was "not whether a university can be Christian, but whether a church exists sufficient to sustain a Christian university."[2] Hauerwas's question highlights the fact that denominations content to function without a richly textured theological tradition will likely never sponsor schools that move much beyond the category of church-relatedness, even though they may call their colleges "Christian."

The second part of my thesis takes the form of a paradox and is meant to explore the kind of theological framework that can sustain a genuinely Christian college or university. On the one hand, I want to argue that church-related education is most deeply Christian when it reflects a radical commitment to Christian discipleship. On the other hand, I want to argue that church-related education is most deeply Christian when it reflects a radical commitment to diversity, pluralism, and genuine academic freedom, and grounds that commitment in a Christian vision of reality.

In fact, I will bracket this discussion with reference to two books that, on the face of things, seem to stand poles apart from one another. One is Lee Camp's *Mere Discipleship,* an uncompromising call for cross-centered living in the twenty-first century. The other is Daniel Taylor's *The Myth of Certainty,* a book that seems to undermine radical claims of any sort, including Camp's embrace of what he calls "radical Christianity." But I am convinced that these two books, together, provide a wonderful basis for answering the question, "What makes church-related education Christian?"

2. Stanley Hauerwas, *With the Grain of the Universe: The Church's Witness and Natural Theology* (Grand Rapids: Brazos Press, 2001), p. 233.

Orienting Ourselves Theologically

I want now to illustrate my thesis by exploring two theological traditions that, yoked together, have the potential to sustain a seriously Christian college or university. Both those traditions descend from the sixteenth century. One is the theological perspective of Martin Luther. The other is the theological perspective of the sixteenth-century Anabaptists.

I recognize that in advancing both Luther and the Anabaptists in the context of an institution's sense of vocation, I am advancing the same two traditions that have shaped my own personal sense of vocation, as I explained in the preface to this book. For this reason, a caveat is now in order. I would not claim that church-related colleges, in order to be authentically Christian, must embrace either Luther or the Anabaptists. But I would suggest that a church-related college that seeks to become authentically Christian must embrace what these two traditions *represent*, namely, a strong theology of justification, on the one hand, and a strong theology of sanctification, on the other. To lift up Luther and the Anabaptists at this point will help us gain a better grasp of how these two themes might work in connected ways in the context of authentically Christian higher education.

Historically, however, Christians have had a difficult time yoking these two themes together. Luther and the Anabaptists furnish only the most obvious case in point. Their quarrels were so intense that the Anabaptists often viewed Luther as a compromiser and no serious Christian at all. For his part, Luther thought the Anabaptists had embraced a doctrine of works righteousness that essentially nullified the good news of the Christian gospel. In addition, Luther viewed their rejection of the state church as fundamentally seditious. He therefore joined Zwingli, Calvin, and the Catholic hierarchy in calling for their destruction.

Yet, Luther and the Anabaptists shared one thing in common: they both were profoundly radical. Historians often single out the

Anabaptists as the true "radicals" of the Reformation, but Luther could hardly have been more radical when he pressed his position to the wall with statements like this:

> Then do we do nothing and work nothing in order to obtain this righteousness? I reply: Nothing at all. For this righteousness means to do nothing, to hear nothing, and to know nothing about the Law or about works but to know and believe only this: that Christ . . . is our High Priest, interceding for us and reigning over us and in us through grace.[3]

Luther even suggested that "should he [a Christian] grow so foolish . . . as to presume to become righteous, free, saved, and a Christian by means of some good work, he would instantly lose faith and all its benefits."[4]

The fact is that Luther claimed the doctrine of justification by grace through faith in the most radical way possible, while the Anabaptists claimed the doctrine of sanctification in the most radical way possible. It is hardly any wonder that these two traditions have been at odds for the better part of 500 years.

While the divorce between Luther and the Anabaptists is hardly surprising, it also stands as one of the greatest tragedies in the history of the Reformation. For that rupture was more than a divorce between two Christian movements. The split between Luther and the Anabaptists also meant that the seamless robe of the gospel was torn in two. For 500 years Luther and his heirs have carefully nurtured the doctrine of justification by grace through faith, while the heirs of the Anabaptists have made discipleship the hallmark of a truly meaningful faith.

3. Martin Luther, *Lectures on Galatians*, 1535, in Jaroslav Pelikan, ed., *Luther's Works*, vol. 26 (Saint Louis: Concordia Publishing House, 1963), p. 8.

4. Luther, *Freedom of a Christian*, 1520, in Harold Grimm, ed., *Luther's Works*, vol. 31 (Philadelphia: Fortress Press, 1957), p. 356.

When all is said and done, however, the doctrine of justification and the doctrine of sanctification are two sides of the same Christian gospel. Luther's advice to "sin boldly" and the Anabaptists' advice to "take up one's cross" are complementary expressions of the same Christian tradition. Luther's insistence that no one can possibly be good enough to save one's self squares beautifully, if paradoxically, with the emphasis the Anabaptists placed on a lifestyle of radically selfless living.

Lest one imagine that the split between Luther and the Anabaptists might have been avoided had each side been content to moderate its claims and embrace a more conservative version of its message, let it be said that both were right in pressing their respective emphases in bold and compelling ways. The doctrine that Christians are justified by grace through faith is an incredibly radical claim, and Luther would have done that doctrine a gross disservice had he preached it with moderation. Likewise, the Christian call to sanctification is a radical demand for cross-centered living. Had the Anabaptists turned that demand into the suggestion that Christians embrace cross-centered lives merely *up to a point,* or had they sought to conform that doctrine to the cultural norms of a fallen empire, they would have lost entirely the meaning of the biblical doctrine of sanctification.

I am suggesting, then, that both these themes — justification and sanctification — are all-or-nothing propositions. But the fact that they are all-or-nothing propositions means that, when yoked together as they are in the Christian gospel, they form an extraordinary paradox. I am also suggesting that these two sides of the Christian paradox, if embraced simultaneously, can provide the strongest possible foundation for a church-related college or university to live out its Christian commitments in a consistent and holistic way.

What would this suggestion look like if implemented on the ground? I want to explore that question by taking up, first, the doctrine of sanctification and, second, the doctrine of justification by grace through faith.

Sanctification and Cross-Centered Living

The biblical understanding of sanctification leads inevitably to the notion of discipleship — even radical discipleship — for the call to sanctification is not a summons to "be nice" or to "be moral" or to "be respectable." Rather, the call to sanctification is a summons to cross-centered living.

David Lipscomb, the Anabaptist-like nineteenth-century leader of Churches of Christ and co-founder of the school that eventually became Lipscomb University in Nashville, Tennessee, put it well when he wrote, "There is no doubt the devil is willing to turn moral reformer and make the world moral and respectable." But from Lipscomb's perspective, morality and respectability were insufficient. Instead, Lipscomb claimed, the New Testament advocates "a full surrender of the soul, mind, and body up to God," leading to "the spirit of self-denial, of self-sacrifice, the forbearance [sic] and long suffering, [and] the doing good for evil."[5]

Samuel S. Hill Jr. — the dean of historians of religion in the American South who labored for most of his career in the University of North Carolina and the University of Florida — told me once that, in his view, church-related higher education could become once more a powerful force in American life. But for that to happen, he said, Christian colleges and universities would have to be less content to be merely church-related and more concerned to recover the radical implications of the Christian gospel.

What might it mean to recover the radical implications of the Christian gospel?

To help answer this question, I want to turn to Lee Camp's insightful book, *Mere Discipleship: Radical Christianity in a Rebellious World*. Camp argues that Christians practiced a radical form of faithfulness to the teachings of Jesus for the first 300 years of Chris-

---

5. David Lipscomb, *Civil Government*, 1889 (Nashville: Gospel Advocate, 1957), pp. 144-45.

tian history. They shared their possessions with those in need, rejected violence, and sought to live out the values of the Upside-Down Kingdom.

But all that changed in the fourth century when Constantine legalized the Christian faith and when Theodosius made Christianity the official religion of the Roman Empire. From that time on, the church served the empire even as the empire protected the church, and the notion of radical discipleship — with precious few exceptions — was lost.

Camp argues that while the Constantinian compromise is ancient history, many American Christians nonetheless view the world through a "Constantinian cataract."[6] Many, for example, view themselves as *American* Christians whose first allegiance is to the United States, rather than as Christians who happen to live in the United States and whose first allegiance is not to America but to the kingdom of God.

For such Christians, "empire" defines reality, Jesus and his teachings become impractical and irrelevant to the "real world," and serious discipleship essentially disappears. Christians who define their identity in terms of empire, Camp argues, inevitably serve the goal of self-preservation. They therefore trust in the power of the state, the power of the market, and the power of the sword, rather than in the power of the cross that requires disciples to abandon themselves for the sake of the neighbor, even if the neighbor proves to be an enemy.

On the other hand, radical discipleship means that Christians render to the kingdom of God their complete and unqualified allegiance, even if that allegiance entails suffering. For Christians who find the notion of suffering unsettling, Camp points out time and again that the cross — not power and privilege — defines the kingdom of God.

6. Lee Camp, *Mere Discipleship: Radical Christianity in a Rebellious World* (Grand Rapids: Brazos Press, 2003), p. 21.

From this perspective, Camp explores the biblical meaning of nonviolence. "Christians refuse to fight wars," he explains, "not because they naively believe they will thus rid the world of war; instead, we do not fight wars because the kingdom of God has come, in which war is banished, in which it is possible to order our lives according to the justice and peace of God. Christian non-violence, then, is always rooted in the narrative of redemption."[7]

In that context, Camp explores what he calls "the political meaning of baptism." In baptism, Camp explains, "Christians become part of a community that transcends all racial, cultural, national, geographical, and natural boundaries." Conversely, "the god of 'God and country' does not baptize into the Spirit of Christ, but the spirit of homeland security; this god baptizes not in the blood of the Lamb, but the blood of soil and country."[8]

Even a cursory reading of American history reveals the extent to which American Christians have often viewed the world through the "Constantinian cataract" that Camp describes. In the nineteenth century, for example, Frederick Douglass, the noted abolitionist and former slave, argued that American Christianity had so thoroughly conformed itself to the norms of the broader culture, and especially the norm of slavery, that it no longer resembled the teachings of Jesus. In 1845, as he concluded his autobiography, Douglass wrote the following words:

> Between the Christianity of this land, and the Christianity of Christ, I recognize the widest possible difference — so wide, that to receive the one as good, pure, and holy, is of necessity to reject the other as bad, corrupt, and wicked. To be the friend of the one, is of necessity to be the enemy of the other. I love the pure, peaceable, and impartial Christianity of Christ; I therefore hate the corrupt, slaveholding, women-whipping,

7. Camp, *Mere Discipleship,* p. 127.
8. Camp, *Mere Discipleship,* p. 145.

§ *The Vocation of the Christian Scholar*

cradle-plundering, partial and hypocritical Christianity of this land. Indeed, I can see no reason, but the most deceitful one, for calling the religion of this land Christianity. I look upon it as the climax of all misnomers, the boldest of all frauds, and the grossest of all libels.

And then, so no one could imagine his quarrel was with southern churches only, Douglass concluded, "Dark and terrible as is this picture, I hold it to be strictly true of the overwhelming mass of professed Christians in America."[9]

One hundred and eighteen years later, Martin Luther King Jr. picked up on the very same theme. In his "Letter from a Birmingham Jail," King lamented the extent to which Christianity in the American South had become little more than a reflection of cultural tradition. "In the midst of blatant injustices inflicted upon the Negro," he wrote, "I have watched white churches stand on the sideline and merely mouth pious irrelevancies and sanctimonious trivialities. In the midst of a mighty struggle to rid our nation of racial and economic injustice, I have heard so many ministers say, 'Those are social issues with which the gospel has no real concern.'" Then King wrote,

On sweltering summer days and crisp autumn mornings I have looked at [the] . . . beautiful churches [of the South] with their lofty spires pointing heavenward. I have beheld the impressive outlay of her massive religious education buildings. Over and over again I have found myself asking: "What kind of people worship here? Who is their God? Where were their voices when the lips of Governor Barnett dripped with words of interposition and nullification? Where were they when Governor Wallace gave the clarion call for defiance and

9. Frederick Douglass, *Narrative of the Life of Frederick Douglass, An American Slave, Written By Himself,* 1845 (New York: Signet Books, 1968), pp. 120-21.

hatred? Where were their voices of support when tired, bruised and weary Negro men and women decided to rise from the dark dungeons of complacency to the bright hills of creative protest?"[10]

For King, radical Christianity didn't conform to the values of the culture; it conformed itself to the mandates of the gospel, and on the basis of the gospel, stood in judgment on the culture with its moral and ethical compromises.

The question we now must raise is this: what does this extended discussion of radical Christianity have to do with church-related higher education? We can answer that question by asking another: if King had examined the church-related institutions of higher learning in the South — schools like Mercer, Xavier, Furman, Samford, Lipscomb, Rhodes, Baylor, Davidson, Harding, Hendrix, Southern Methodist, Wesleyan, or Abilene Christian — would he have judged those institutions in the same way that he judged their sponsoring churches?

I can tell you this. I was an undergraduate student at a church-related institution in the South between 1961 and 1965. For all those years, I was no more than 250 miles from most of the great events of the Freedom Movement. The lunch counter sit-ins had begun the year before I entered college and continued throughout my undergraduate years. In 1963, midway through my undergraduate experience, Martin Luther King led hundreds of children through the streets of Birmingham, protesting racial segregation. The city responded with fire hoses and police dogs. In 1965, the year I graduated from college, blacks sought to march across the Edmund Pettus Bridge from Selma to Montgomery, but Alabama storm troopers stopped them in their tracks with shockingly brutal force.

10. Martin Luther King Jr., "Letter from a Birmingham Jail," in James M. Washington, ed., *I Have a Dream: Writings and Speeches that Changed the World* (San Francisco: HarperSanFrancisco, 1986), pp. 96-97.

Unbelievably, in spite of the fact that one of the greatest moral dramas in the history of the United States was unfolding under my nose, I missed it. I missed it almost entirely. I didn't fully discover what I had missed until I enrolled as a graduate student at the University of Iowa in 1967. I blame myself, but I also blame that church-related college and its professors, for not one of my teachers said to me, "What is going on today is important. Take note." Or better still, "Get involved."

Should my professors have encouraged me to take the Freedom Movement seriously? Should they have urged me to participate? Given the purposes of higher education — and Christian higher education in particular — could it have been their rightful role to encourage in my classmates and me an openness — even a commitment — to the claims of discipleship in the context of the Freedom Movement? Could it have been their rightful role to encourage us to judge the culture by the light of the Christian gospel instead of the other way around?

It is well enough to talk about issues like slavery in the nineteenth century or the Freedom Movement that took place almost half a century ago, but the real question for us is this: What is our responsibility as teachers when faced with comparable moral issues today? For example, do we engage our students in an exploration of how the Christian faith might bear on the war in Iraq? Do we help them explore what the Christian faith might say regarding war and violence in any context at all? In a culture where a majority of students are chiefly concerned with making money and living the good life, do we encourage our students to embrace the values of the Upside-Down Kingdom? Do we counsel them to take Jesus seriously when he told us to lose ourselves for the sake of others; when he told us to invite to dinner the poor, the maim, and the blind; when he told us to die in order to live; or when he told us to take up the cross and follow him? Do we explore with our students what all this might mean in the context of their lives and their vocations?

On the other hand, has the Constantinian cataract so obscured our vision that our practice of Christian higher education has been chiefly shaped by our allegiance to the empire rather than to the kingdom of God?

Someone might well ask, "What possible justification could there be for bringing a consideration of discipleship and sanctification into our classrooms?" We can answer that question easily enough.

Over the past twenty years, many scholars in church-related colleges and universities have concluded that Christian faith and secular learning should, indeed, connect in significant ways. The dominant paradigm for that connection has increasingly become the integrationist model that calls for the "integration of faith and learning."

As good as that model may be, it has its deficiencies. In an important book called *Teaching Peace,* produced in large part by Mennonite scholars at Bluffton College, Gerald Biesecker-Mast argues that the integrationist model is deficient in part because it begins with the creation rather than with the life and teachings of Jesus. It can therefore sidestep the radical claims of the Christian gospel, and can do so quite easily. Precisely for that reason, as Biesecker-Mast explains, the integrationist model "is usually mobilized on behalf of conservative rather than liberationist social agendas, sometimes explicitly rejecting the more radical Anabaptist critiques of social and political systems."[11]

In another important book — *Scholarship and Christian Faith: Enlarging the Conversation* — Rodney Sawatsky, president of Messiah College, argues that when proponents of the integrationist model speak of faith and learning, they typically narrow "their definition of faith to mean religious *beliefs about* God, the world, and humankind, or a *worldview* embracing all these ideas" (italics mine).

---

11. Gerald Biesecker-Mast, "Christian Nonviolence and the Enlightenment Crisis," in J. Denny Weaver and Gerald Biesecker-Mast, eds., *Teaching Peace: Nonviolence and the Liberal Arts* (New York: Rowman and Littlefield, 2003), p. 7.

But what about "faith as a verb"? Sawatsky asks perceptively. What about "faith understood as trust" or faith understood as "'seeking and discovering meaning'"? And what about "hope" and "love"? After all, he notes, "The Apostle Paul used three words to describe the full contours of Christian identity: faith, hope, and love." Sawatsky then argues that in addition to integrating learning with faith understood as a noun, Christian scholars should also integrate learning with hope, with love, and with faith understood as trust or a search for meaning.[12]

In this highly suggestive passage, Sawatsky offers a powerful rationale for integrating the virtues of faith, hope, and love into our teaching and our scholarship. He thereby provides us with compelling reasons for teaching discipleship, sanctification, and cross-centered living, even as we teach history, literature, anthropology, and physics.

To this point in our discussion of sanctification, however, we have told only half the story. The second part of the story — every bit as critical as the first — pertains not so much to teachers and scholars as to high-level administrators and development officials at church-related colleges and universities and to the way they market their institutions.

It is not uncommon for faculty members at these colleges and universities to work diligently at connecting their teaching and their scholarship with Christian faith and discipleship, while the development staff pulls the institution in completely different directions. This can happen, for example, when a school seeks to market itself as a Democratic institution or a Republican institution as opposed to a Christian institution, or when development officers confuse the way of the cross with American ideals, nationalism, and patriotism.

There is a great deal of money to be raised from people who

12. Rodney J. Sawatsky, "Prologue: The Virtue of Scholarly Hope," in Douglas Jacobsen and Rhonda Hustedt Jacobsen, eds., *Scholarship & Christian Faith: Enlarging the Conversation* (New York: Oxford University Press, 2004), p. 4.

think of the United States as a Christian nation and who confuse discipleship with patriotism, but the church-related college or university that embarks on that path does so at the risk of great peril. The fact is, my own undergraduate institution — the church-related school that did such a good job of sheltering my colleagues and me from the Civil Rights Movement — held as its official motto the phrase "Where Christian and American ideals go hand in hand." Is there not irony here?

The fact is, Christian and American ideals are often incompatible. The liberty that the Declaration of Independence holds to be an "unalienable right," for example, is often construed as the liberty to pursue one's own self-interest, while liberty in the context of Christian faith is the liberty *from* self-interest and the freedom to give one's self away. Capitalism values acquisition, places a premium on greed, and encourages citizens to say of their possessions, "This is mine." Christian faith, on the other hand, maintains that all things are God's, that nothing is finally "ours," that we are only stewards of the earth, and that we must share the wealth that comes into our hands with those less fortunate than ourselves. One could go on and on with the contrasts between American ideals and institutions and the meaning of the Christian call to discipleship.

In spite of these contrasts, however, some church-related schools sell themselves as schools that are committed to a predominantly American vision of reality, and some colleges and universities that market themselves as Christian institutions still court donors who confuse the Christian faith with the American way of life. The crucial consideration here is that donors, quite understandably, typically give with the expectation that the institution that receives their gift will embrace their values. To that extent, all institutions are donor-driven.

An undergraduate student once told me that she had been invited to make a report to a group of donors who gave generously to an unnamed church-related college. She was shocked to hear these donors insist that the school in question recruit "more Republican students" and "make the school a bastion for conservative politics." One might wish that those donors had argued for more Christian students who were willing to embrace the biblical call to discipleship.

In order to be true to its mission, it is crucial that a Christian institution find donors who share the values of the gospel, rather than donors who bring a perspective alien to the gospel and who seek to shape the institution according to their own ideological commitments.

In our attempt to answer the question, "What makes church-related education Christian?" we have focused to this point on one side of the Christian paradox — the doctrine of sanctification — and we have explored that doctrine's implications for teaching, for scholarship, and for institutional development. Now we must turn to the other side of the Christian paradox — the doctrine of justification by grace through faith.

Justification by Grace through Faith and the Mandate for Diversity, Pluralism, and Academic Freedom

In the introductory section of this chapter, I stated the following:

> I want to argue that church-related education is most deeply Christian when it reflects a radical commitment to Christian discipleship. On the other hand, I want to argue that church-related education is most deeply Christian when it reflects a radical commitment to diversity, pluralism, and genuine academic freedom, and grounds that commitment in a Christian vision of reality.

The Christian vision of reality in which church-related colleges and universities can ground their commitment to diversity, pluralism, and academic freedom is, quite simply, the biblical doctrine of justification by grace through faith. That doctrine presupposes two important themes.

First, it presupposes that God alone is God. He is the infinite Lord of heaven and earth, the one whose love no one can fathom and whose goodness and greatness no one can comprehend.

Second, it presupposes that human beings, while made in God's image, are nonetheless finite, frail, and subject to extraordinary limitations — limitations underscored by the fact that death is a fundamental and inescapable dimension of human life. Our finitude means, among other things, that our knowledge is limited and our understanding is flawed, simply by virtue of the fact that we are human beings, confined to a particular time and a particular place. Even if we were to expand our horizons through study and travel, we would never completely overcome the limitations that define our lives. Not only this, but greed and self-interest — traits that define the meaning of sin — inevitably cloud our vision and limit both the scope and accuracy of our perception. Given these extraordinary limitations, how could we possibly imagine that we could save ourselves?

These two themes — the sovereignty of the infinite God and the finitude of humankind — give meaning to the doctrine of justification by grace through faith. God has said "yes" to us by virtue of his infinite love and grace. We are asked to accept that grace through the light of faith.

These two themes — the sovereignty of the infinite God and the finitude of humankind — also provide the strongest possible motivation for a Christian college or university to embrace diversity, pluralism, and academic freedom.

If it is true that our knowledge is limited and our understanding flawed simply by virtue of time and place, and if it is true that greed and self-interest inevitably cloud our vision and limit the scope of our perception, then who are we to insist that we alone have a corner on the market of truth? Who are we to assume that other human beings from other cultures, from other periods in human history, from other political persuasions and other religions may not have perceptions and understandings fully as valid as our own?

This consideration means that of all educational institutions,

Christian colleges and universities stand under a mandate to embrace diversity and pluralism and to extend to their faculties the freedom to search, to think, and to explore, even when those explorations threaten our sense of self and render us less than comfortable. This is precisely why I wish to argue that church-related education is most deeply Christian when it reflects a radical commitment to diversity, pluralism, and genuine academic freedom and grounds that commitment in a Christian vision of reality.

Daniel Taylor, in his remarkable book, *The Myth of Certainty*, sheds abundant light on this issue. As a young man growing up in a fundamentalist church, Taylor discovered, much to his chagrin, that his fellow Christians typically prized both certainty and orthodoxy, and prized them in oppressive ways. He struggled with the fact that he was not allowed to question the church, its beliefs, or its practices. He discovered that "questioning the institution . . . [was] synonymous, for many, with attacking God."[13]

Years later as a graduate student, and then as a young professor, he discovered the same oppressive reality in the context of the American academy, except the academy substituted secular orthodoxies for religious orthodoxies. Further, he discovered that those who embraced those secular orthodoxies often punished those who dared to question their legitimacy. "Reflecting critically on secularist orthodoxy," he wrote, "will draw just as much fire in this world, which supposedly prizes reflection, as questioning religious orthodoxy will in the other."[14]

Warned of orthodoxies that must never be questioned and truths that must never be doubted, Taylor embarked on a long, intense struggle with the entire question of certainty. He shares both the struggle and the conclusions he finally reached in his book, *The Myth of Certainty*.

13. Daniel Taylor, *The Myth of Certainty* (Downers Grove, Ill.: InterVarsity Press, 1986), p. 30.
14. Taylor, *The Myth of Certainty*, p. 49.

His essential conclusion, as the title of the book suggests, is that certainty is, indeed, a myth, especially when certainty pertains to absolutes. "Absolutes, by definition, partake of infinity," he writes. "They are without boundary. What relationship can a finite knower have with an infinite object of knowledge except a finite, limited one? Can one then be said to know or 'have' an absolute on which to ground one's beliefs when one only knows, at best, a sliver of that absolute?"[15]

Indeed, Taylor makes a strong case for radical skepticism.

> The reflective Christian does well, in my view, to freely admit the possibility of being wrong. All I believe in may in fact be false. God may be only wish fulfillment. The sense of His presence that I sometimes get in worship and prayer may derive simply from the release of certain chemicals in the brain. Those occasions where He seems to have guided my life may only be coincidence or reflect my human desire to find a pattern in events.[16]

On reading a passage like this, someone might well ask in what sense Taylor can claim to be Christian at all. If he is willing freely to "admit the possibility of being wrong" and seriously to entertain the notion that even his belief in God "may be only wish fulfillment," how on earth can Taylor claim any credible Christian allegiance whatsoever?

In response, Taylor writes that his Christian convictions rest not on certainty, but on faith. What is this, but an affirmation of the historic Christian doctrine that we are justified by grace through faith, and not by works, knowledge, or certainty? "Faith," he writes, "is a quality and a choice consistent with the riskiness of the human condition. It is an appropriate response to the world as I find it."[17] Put

15. Taylor, *The Myth of Certainty*, p. 91.
16. Taylor, *The Myth of Certainty*, p. 97.
17. Taylor, *The Myth of Certainty*, p. 98.

another way, Taylor embraces his finitude. What else can he do? Indeed, if we admit that our vision is clouded and distorted by time and place, self-interest and greed, what else can anyone do?

Taylor's assertion that "the reflective Christian does well . . . to freely admit the possibility of being wrong," strikes me as a modern counterpart to Luther's confident assertion that the Christian will inevitably sin. Luther advised his followers to accept their humanity, their finitude, and their brokenness, and therefore to "sin boldly." In like manner, Taylor counsels Christians to accept the fact that final certitude is a myth and therefore to doubt boldly, since doubt is the inevitable counterpart of faith.

"There is no more honest expression of the tension of faith," Taylor claims, "than that of the distraught father in the gospel of Mark seeking healing for his child. To Jesus' assertion that belief makes all things possible, the father cries out in tears, 'Lord, I believe; help thou my unbelief.'"[18] In Taylor's judgment, this distraught father is a stand-in for every man and every woman who faces the question of certainty about ultimate things.

Taylor concludes his book with this assertion.

> The goal of faith is not to create a set of immutable, rationalized, precisely defined and defendable beliefs to preserve forever. It is to recover a relationship with God. . . . As a belief system, the Christian religion is subject to the many ills of all belief systems; as an encounter with God, it transforms individual lives and human history. God does not give us primarily a belief system; he gives us Himself, most clearly in the person of Jesus Christ, so that truth and meaning can be ours through a commitment to that love with which He first loved us. The risk is great, but the reward is infinite.[19]

18. Taylor, *The Myth of Certainty*, p. 98.
19. Taylor, *The Myth of Certainty*, pp. 123-24.

Michael Himes eloquently describes this same issue by comparing Christian scholars to Jacob who wrestled with the angel throughout the night. Himes notes, "The end of the story of Jacob's night of wrestling with God is that he left the Jordan bank limping because of his shattered hip (Gen. 32:32). What a perfect image! Jacob goes limping across the Jordan into the promised land, and the limp is the proof that he has now become Israel." Then Himes makes the crucial point.

> We must be willing to share the story of our limp with others by admitting in our teaching, in our relationships, in our service of others that we have not got a perfect and finished grasp of the truth but are eager to continue the struggle to clarify our partial vision. We may never find fully adequate answers, but the fight to find the answers is worth everything. For it is in the tangle of the mind that we become truly human and therefore also truly and authentically Christian. And the sign of that is that we approach the promised land limping.[20]

We now must ask, what does this discussion of doubt, faith, and certitude have to do with the task of Christian education? How does it contribute to any meaningful answer to the question, "What makes church-related education Christian?" And finally, how does it relate to the other half of the Christian paradox, the demand for radical discipleship?

Already, I have suggested that a frank acceptance of our radical finitude, and the frank acceptance of the fact that we are justified not by works or knowledge or wisdom, but by God's infinite grace, is a powerful foundation — and a profoundly Christian foundation — on which a Christian college can build an institutional commitment to diversity, pluralism, and academic freedom.

20. Michael J. Himes, *Doing the Truth in Love: Conversations About God, Relationships and Service* (New York: Paulist Press, 1995), p. 62.

Second, a frank acceptance of our radical finitude, and the frank acceptance of the fact that we are justified not by works or knowledge or wisdom, but by God's infinite grace, should make us cautious about dogmatisms of every kind, even dogmatisms regarding radical discipleship. We live by the light of faith, and what may be clear to me may not be so clear to my brother or my sister.

Further, recognition of our finitude should make us sensitive to the ambiguity of the human situation. No situation is ideal and no circumstance is perfect. This is a profoundly Christian teaching, and a teaching that means, quite frankly, that the Christian must be prepared for compromise. For example, the Christian institution that seeks to identify donors who are fully in sync with the institution's mission may find donors who are on board in certain ways but not in others.

The wise administrator, the wise development officer, will have to make a determination regarding how much compromise the institution can tolerate in a given situation, while still maintaining the integrity of the institutional mission. But the genius of the wise and committed administrator of a Christian college or university is this: he or she will always chart the vessel's course by asking, "How does this or that decision square with the basic theological convictions that undergird this institution? How does it square with the institution's commitment to discipleship? How does it square with our confidence in the grace of almighty God?"

These conclusions, in turn, should cause those associated with Christian higher education carefully to nurture a profound sense of humility regarding our work and to avoid at all costs any hint of triumphalism. After all, Christian schools, like all human institutions, are fundamentally flawed. What makes the difference in Christian higher education are the commitments that undergird and inform our work — the commitment to a radical sense of discipleship and the commitment to the good news that God's love sustains us even in the midst of our failures.

Conclusions

If acceptance of our finitude and recognition of the ambiguity of the human situation should make us cautious about dogmatisms and open even to compromise in certain situations, why then would I say — as I did say earlier in this essay — that the Christian doctrines of radical discipleship and justification by grace through faith are, each of them, all-or-nothing propositions?

The truth is, they *are* all-or-nothing propositions, and precisely here we find the paradox of the Christian gospel. The demand for radical discipleship is a categorical imperative, to be sure, but it never cancels out the absolute message of grace. Paul makes this point when he tells the Galatians, "All who rely on observing the law are under a curse, for it is written: 'Cursed is everyone who does not continue to do everything written in the Book of the Law.' Clearly no one is justified before God by the law, because, 'The righteous will live by faith'" (3:10-11).

At the same time, the absolute reality of God's grace does not constitute license to ignore the categorical imperative to discipleship. After his tribute to the power of grace, Paul then asked the Roman Christians what really amounted to a rhetorical question.

> What shall we say, then? Shall we go on sinning so that grace may increase? By no means! We died to sin; how can we live in it any longer? Or don't you know that all of us who were baptized into Christ Jesus were baptized into his death? We were therefore buried with him through baptism into death in order that, just as Christ was raised from the dead through the glory of the Father, we too may live a new life. (6:1-4)

The truth is, the gospel *is* a radical message. It is radical in its call for discipleship and radical in its promise of grace. But grace apart from discipleship can be "cheap," and discipleship apart from grace can quickly degenerate into legalism. This is why sanctification *and* justification are the two indispensable poles of the paradox of the Christian gospel, and the two indispensable dimensions of Christian higher education.

When the board, the administration, and the faculty of a church-related college or university can embrace this paradox and orient the institution squarely in the context of these imperatives, that institution ceases to be merely church-related. It becomes, instead, deeply and profoundly Christian.

129

Tragedy, Christian Faith, and the Life of the Mind: Personal Reflections

I HAVE ARGUED ON VIRTUALLY EVERY PAGE OF THIS BOOK THAT IF we seek to grow into first-rate scholars — scholars who can celebrate diversity and multiple points of view, scholars who can listen carefully to the voices of other human beings, scholars who can ask critical questions without foreclosing prematurely with simplistic answers — if we seek to grow into scholars who are genuinely thoughtful and reflective, then we must take several crucial steps. We must take upon ourselves the ambiguity that inevitably defines the human situation. We must embrace our finitude and be quick to acknowledge our very deep-seated limitations. And we must develop paradoxical ways of thinking and living so that we can listen for deep and lasting truths in opposing points of view.

Here, in this final chapter, I want to suggest that as we seek to achieve these objectives, tragedy can be an ironic kind of friend. Clearly, few of us would voluntarily welcome tragedy and suffering into our lives. Nonetheless, if we are willing to embrace those unwelcome guests and explore the lessons they can teach, we may well discover — in spite of ourselves — some truths that are simply fundamental to first-class teaching and scholarship. For tragedy and suffering can teach us, as nothing else can, what it really means to be human: that life is ambiguous and frail and that finitude is the defining characteristic of human existence.

If we respond to the tragic dimensions of human life with the rich resources of the Christian faith, we may also learn what it means to live in the midst of paradox. For the Christian faith can help us see that life is a continuous round of "yes" and "no," of tragedy and reclamation, of death and redemption. And so I am suggesting, here in this final chapter, that tragedy and Christian conviction, yoked together, can provide the Christian scholar with incomparable resources to sustain the life of the mind.

Tragedy, Christian Faith, and the Life of the Mind: The Story of Gerrit J. tenZythoff

Gerrit tenZythoff served as chairperson of the Department of Religious Studies at Southwest Missouri State University from 1969 to 1983, and continued to teach in that department until 1992 when he retired. There is no way I could have known, when I joined the religious studies faculty at SMSU in 1977, the ways this man would shape my life. And though I taught there for only six years, that was ample time for Gerrit to teach me some of the most important lessons I have ever learned.

Thanks to devout Christian parents who encouraged in their young son convictions common to the Reformed wing of the Christian tradition, Gerrit tenZythoff had developed a meaningful sense of vocation long before May of 1940 when the Nazis invaded his native Holland. It was precisely that sense of vocation that allowed him to respond to Nazi brutality with astounding courage and conviction. That response, in turn, both deepened and defined his sense of vocation, providing guidance, direction, and calling for the rest of his life.

Like many of their Christian neighbors, the tenZythoff family hid Jews from the prying eyes and the brutal hands of Nazi soldiers. Gerrit was still in his teens at the time, but though he was very young, he was determined to do his part in the resistance.

The occasion to implement that resistance occurred when the

Nazis ordered Jewish teachers and Jewish students out of Gerrit's high school. In addition, all books written by Jews would be confiscated. In protest, the students went on strike and adamantly refused to sign the oath of loyalty to the German regime that now occupied the Netherlands. In reprisal, the Nazis closed the universities and arrested the students, Gerrit among them.

The Nazis took Gerrit to a forced labor camp in Berlin. There, they demanded that he reveal the names of friends and neighbors who were sheltering Jews. Gerrit refused to tell. As he later said, "I would rather die than tell any of the names that I knew." The Nazis, however, believed that Gerrit would buckle under torture. So several prison guards held him horizontally and rammed him, head first and repeatedly, into a brick wall. Still, Gerrit refused to divulge the names. He paid a heavy price for that decision, a price that would cause him to suffer in a variety of ways for the rest of his life.

In September of 1943, Allied bombers scored a direct hit on the prison where the Nazis were holding Gerrit captive. That strike created such confusion in the prison that Gerrit walked free, though the risk he now faced was the fact that he had no valid identification papers. Without those papers, he could be shot on sight. So at a nearby railway station, he picked up some Nazi propaganda, material that he held on his chest while he raised his hand high and mouthed that despicable phrase, "Heil, Hitler," when he encountered Nazi soldiers. In this way, he made his way back to his native Holland.

When the war was over, he was finally free to return to his parents' home. There, he found two children he had never seen before. When he learned their names, he was furious. "What?" he protested. "They're Nazis!" "Yes," his parents said, "their parents were Nazis." "Then I don't want to be under the same roof with those bastards," Gerrit yelled, and he walked out the back door. Immediately, his mother came after him and spoke words that reinforced his sense of vocation. "You are wrong, Gerrit," she said. "You and we are not Nazis. We are Christians, and we will stand with the innocent."

In 1992, Gerrit told this story to a rapt convocation audience at

Pepperdine University. It was a story he had seldom told during all those years. On this particular occasion, however, he wished to address the topic "Am I My Brother's Keeper?" His willingness to tell this story on that occasion allowed him to address his topic with extraordinary power.

During the course of that speech, he told the students that his worst memory was not the torture the Nazis inflicted on him in the prison camp in Berlin. Instead, his worst memories were those occasions when Nazi soldiers engaged in a "search of the house." When the Nazis found children in the house, they always asked them to pray. Routinely, the Jewish children — anxious to show that they could say their prayers — would begin, "Baruch Atah Adonai." And they were taken away to be killed. Then, with an aching pain in his voice that reflected his deep sensitivity to people of cultural and religious traditions different from his own, Gerrit recalled, "We had to teach them to say, 'Our Father who art in heaven.' Why was that the worst memory? Because we had to make something out of them that they were not. And nobody ought to undergo that experience."

Why have I chosen to rehearse this portion of Gerrit's story? What could this saga possibly have to do with either Christian faith or the life of the mind? And why has Gerrit tenZythoff emerged as such a compelling, remarkable, and influential figure in my life, ever since I first met him in 1977?

The answer to each of those questions has everything to do with Gerrit's own sense of vocation, reinforced — as I have said — by the way Gerrit responded to the evil he encountered during World War II. Clearly, Gerrit could have responded to these events with bitterness and cynicism, and in this way, he could have become a singularly *un*remarkable man. Instead, Gerrit remained to the end one of the most vibrant, positive, and buoyant people I have ever encountered.

Gerrit was not naïve, for he had seen the face and felt the hands of evil incarnate. And he knew from lived experience that human beings are fully capable of perpetrating unspeakable horrors. At the same time, he routinely gave voice to his conviction that "good will triumph over evil."

How could this be? How could this man embrace in his own life such a remarkable paradox?

We will find our answer to that question in the Christian faith that his parents taught him from the time he was a very small child. Raised in the Dutch Reformed tradition, and true to that heritage, Gerrit had always taken seriously the reality of human sin, greed, and self-interest. At the same time, as a Reformed Christian, he had also believed that the sovereign Lord of the universe has not abandoned his creation but would ultimately prevail over sin, evil, and the devil. It is precisely for this reason that he could conclude his Pepperdine address with this stunning, two-line admonition. "Good *will* triumph over evil," he told the students. "All that you and I must do is suffer."

All that we must do is suffer? What an amazing concept! What could he possibly have meant? The answer lies in Gerrit's commitment to the Christian faith, for according to the gospel, we save our lives when we lose them. Indeed, according to the Christian gospel, life always emerges most completely from the very throes of death. Good *will* triumph over evil. There can be no question about that. But we must join the resistance and be willing to pay the price in both small and significant ways.

Based on what I have said throughout this book, it must be apparent how Gerrit's sense of vocation, nurtured by his Christian convictions, helped sustain him as a scholar and a teacher. In the first place, because Gerrit knew firsthand the power of evil, he also knew firsthand the reality of human finitude. Because he knew that he himself — along with all other human beings — was constantly subject to greed and self-interest, he could hardly afford to indulge himself in dogmatic pronouncements. Instead, his scholarship and his teaching were always characterized by a deep-seated humility that allowed him to take seriously the perspectives of cultural and religious traditions that were radically different from his own.

Second, Gerrit's embrace of a profoundly biblical paradox — the reality of evil, on the one hand, but the promise that God will triumph, on the other — is precisely what enabled him to thrive as a scholar and a teacher in a department of religious studies in a state university. His embrace of that paradox provided him with a strong spiritual foundation that allowed him, in turn, to take multiple and competing perspectives seriously, even when those perspectives seemed in radical conflict with one another.

Samuel S. Hill, the scholar who wrote the foreword to this volume, once observed that apart from spiritual discernment, a paradox can appear as nothing more than a contradiction in terms. Through the lens of the Christian faith, Gerrit tenZythoff refused to reduce a paradox to a contradiction in terms. He refused to view the world in binary categories, to think the world in two, or to indulge himself with the simplistic framework of "either-or." Instead, he listened for the voice of truth wherever that voice could be heard. And he heard that voice in a variety of competing perspectives.

Gerrit died on March 20, 2001, of complications from surgery — the last in a series of surgeries designed to repair his central nervous system, so badly damaged by the brutality he suffered at the hands of Nazi soldiers when he was only a boy.

Comfortable with the reality of human finitude and fully at home in the world of paradox, Gerrit tenZythoff emerged as a remarkable teacher, a remarkable scholar, and a remarkable human being. Now, as I look back on my association with Gerrit from a distance of almost thirty years, I realize that this man provided me with an incomparable model for how Christian faith can sustain the life of the mind.

My Own Encounters with the Face of Death

My own encounters with tragedy emerged as encounters with death itself, though my encounters parallel those of Gerrit tenZythoff in only minimal ways. I have had three of those encounters now, and there is nothing about any of them that one might identify as particularly heroic, moral, or ethical. At the same time, there is no way I can dismiss those encounters as inconsequential. In every instance, they have defined my life, enriched my sense of vocation, sharpened my spiritual vision, and allowed me to understand what it really means to be human, after all. As a result, they have provided me with resources that, if properly employed, can equip me to become a better teacher and a better scholar.

The first encounter caught my wife and me completely by surprise. It was in June of 1998, and Jan and I were on our way to Door County, Wisconsin, for a meeting of the national advisory board of the Institute for the Study of American Evangelicals (ISAE) — an organization of American church historians that gathers every year for strategic planning, scholarship, and mutual interaction among ourselves and our families.

Because the 1997-98 academic year had been an extraordinarily busy term, Jan and I decided that we would go to Door County a week in advance of that meeting, simply to relax and play and spend some precious time in the company of one other.

On the flight from Los Angeles to Chicago, I took with me a book that would play a significant role in my first encounter with the face of death. That book was *Tuesdays with Morrie*.

Morris Schwartz, the subject of this book, taught sociology at Brandeis University for many years. Mitch Albom, who wrote the book, was one of Morrie's students at Brandeis. Morrie directed several independent studies for Mitch, as well as his senior thesis. And they always met on Tuesdays.

Mitch finally graduated and left Brandeis to seek his fame and fortune. Almost twenty years went by and Mitch seldom thought about his old professor, even though the two of them had been extremely close. Then, the newspaper for which Mitch worked went on strike. For several months Mitch had time on his hands.

One night, early in the strike, Mitch was surfing the channels on the tube when suddenly, there on the screen, on "Nightline," being interviewed by Ted Koppel, was his old professor, Morrie. Morrie, it turns out, had Lou Gehrig's disease and was dying. Koppel was asking Morrie what it meant to face one's death; how he coped; and how he found the strength to carry on with what little of his life he had left.

Mitch was so moved by what he saw and heard that he flew back to Boston to reconnect with his old professor, Morrie. He and Morrie decided to hold class every Tuesday for the rest of Morrie's life. But this time the subject wasn't sociology. It was life. The question for this class was simply this: What's important and what's not important when one knows that one must die soon? Or, put another way, what's the meaning of life in the face of one's impending death? These are the questions that Mitch and Morrie explored on those Tuesdays before Morrie finally died. And the book, *Tuesdays with Morrie*, essentially gives a loving and tender transcript of those conversations.

In the months leading up to his death, Morrie gave himself not only to Mitch but also to a host of people who sought him out for counsel and advice. For Morrie had made a decision. Mitch describes that decision like this.

> He would not wither. He would not be ashamed of dying. Instead, he would make death his final project, the center point of his days. Since everyone was going to die, he could be of great value, right? He could be research. A human textbook. *Study me in my slow and patient demise. Watch what happens to me. Learn with me.*[1]

Even in the midst of death, Morrie found a renewed sense of vocation.

1. Mitch Albom, *Tuesdays with Morrie: An Old Man, A Young Man, and Life's Greatest Lesson* (New York: Doubleday, 1997), p. 10.

As our plane touched down at O'Hare Field, I turned the last page of *Tuesdays with Morrie,* and as I did, I cried. The truth is, this book had moved me deeply. But through my tears, I managed to comment to Jan, "I am so glad that we have not had to deal with death or catastrophic illness." Jan's response was quick and pointed. "But our friends have," she said. "Why would we think that we could escape for long?"

Our first three days in Door County were simply magnificent. Jan and I had time to play and time to talk and time to share in ways that the busyness of the previous nine months had made all too rare. Jan still says that on a scale of 1 to 10, she would give those days a 20.

And then, on the evening of Father's Day, a night that we had planned as a special time together, I experienced a crushing pain in my chest and an aching sensation in my right arm. After a night in the regional hospital, I woke up the next morning at Bellin Hospital in Green Bay where the doctors confirmed that I had suffered a heart attack. And they were amazed. I had none of the risk factors, they explained. I was not a smoker, I was not overweight, my cholesterol was only slightly elevated, and I had no history of heart disease in my family. Nonetheless, there I was, hospitalized because my heart had failed me.

As heart attacks go, the doctors explained, this one was mild. Nonetheless, it had stunned the right side of my heart so severely that the right side had simply stopped. For five days, the right side of my heart did virtually nothing at all, forcing the left side to do all the work to sustain my vital functions. For those five days, the intensive care unit at Bellin Hospital became home, both for me and for Jan. Not until my seventh — and last — day in the hospital would we learn the proper medical description for what I had experienced: the heart attack had triggered congestive heart failure.

It occurred to me in the midst of this ordeal that I might never leave Bellin Hospital alive. I had often wondered how I might respond when the time came for me to stare the angel of death in the face. Would I be terrified? Could I handle my impending death with any grace at all?

I was pleasantly surprised when I greeted this experience with an incredible level of tranquility. I knew even then why this was true. I was deeply convicted — and remain convinced — that I am justified and saved by the grace of God, in spite of my countless failings. For many years I have taken great comfort in the promise we find in Romans 8:31-39,

> What, then, shall we say in response to this? If God is for us, who can be against us? . . . Who shall separate us from the love of Christ? Shall trouble or hardship or persecution or famine or nakedness or danger or sword? . . . No, in all these things we are more than conquerors through him who loved us. For I am convinced that neither death nor life, neither angels nor demons, neither the present nor the future, nor any powers, neither height nor depth, nor anything else in all creation, will be able to separate us from the love of God that is in Christ Jesus our Lord.

My conviction of the truth of this promise sustained me throughout this ordeal.

But three other factors contributed to my tranquility in very significant ways. First, my wife, Jan, never left my side. She says, even now, that this was her heart attack, too, and in a very real sense, it was.

Second, there were so many friends. When my ISAE colleagues arrived in Door County and discovered my situation, they came to my bedside every night to share in this ordeal. Beyond this, Jan spent many hours of every day talking by phone to friends who had called from all over the country, simply to wish me well. I never knew I had so many friends, and that knowledge did much to sustain me.

And finally, because that marvelous little book, *Tuesdays with Morrie*, was still so fresh on my mind, I filtered this entire experience through the wisdom that Morrie Schwartz conveyed.

Upon learning of the strategic role that Morrie had played in my ordeal, one of my Jewish colleagues on the Pepperdine faculty asked how it was that I could draw such strength from a man who was a Jew and not a Christian. My answer was simple: Morrie was a human being who faced and dealt with universal human questions in ways that transcend religious differences.

But there is more I could have said to my friend, for Morrie embraced his finitude, took the ambiguity of human life upon himself, and out of the depths of his pain and despair, found the strength to affirm a powerful vision of life. I related to Morrie because, though he was not a Christian, he embraced a way of living and a way of dying that seemed to share much in common with the truths I have learned from the Christian gospel. For Morrie understood that life comes from death, and that those of us who seek to save our lives will surely lose them, but those of us who are prepared to give our lives away will surely find them in the end. In this way, although a Jew and not a Christian, Morrie Schwartz became for me a sacrament of the grace of God and helped sustain me in my hour of peril.

When Jan and I returned to Los Angeles, we paid a visit to Dr. James Lim, my personal physician. Normally jovial and good-natured, on this particular occasion Dr. Lim seemed somber, even stern. "Come into my office," he said, and we did. "Have a seat," he offered, and we complied with that invitation as well. Then he looked me straight in the eye and said tersely, "I want to tell you something." He spoke three short words that I shall never forget. "They saved you," he said. "What are you telling me, doctor?" I asked. "I'm telling you," he responded, "that when someone has a heart attack and congestive heart failure simultaneously, it is very difficult to stabilize that person. And they saved you."

I knew then that for reasons I could not fathom, and in ways I could not understand, God had spared my life. As we left the doctor's office that day, I felt terribly grateful but also terribly vulnerable. Those two sentiments — gratitude and vulnerability — have remained with me ever since.

Then, only two years later, I experienced my second encounter with a life and death issue. In June of 2000, the doctors told me I had prostate cancer. This news did not come as a complete surprise since I know that many men must deal with this disease. Jan and I explored the various options for treatment and finally opted for surgery to remove the prostate altogether. The surgery was successful and the pathology report revealed that the cancer had been confined to that organ. Once again, I felt as if my life had been returned to me, and once again, I felt profoundly grateful but also profoundly vulnerable.

Only two weeks following that surgery, I experienced my third encounter with the face of death. It came in the form of shortness of breath. The doctors advised me not to worry since a certain level of shortness of breath can be expected following a major operation. But after a couple of weeks, the shortness of breath became more severe, so severe in fact that I could not draw enough breath from my lungs to frame a single sentence. At the prompting of dear and precious friends, we rushed to the emergency room where the doctors discovered that blood clots — numerous blood clots — had filled my lungs, choking off my oxygen supply.

The next morning, Dr. Lim — my personal physician — came to the room where I was hospitalized. Dr. Lim was the same physician who had told me two and one-half years before that the doctors at Bellin Hospital in Green Bay, Wisconsin, had saved my life. Once again he spoke words that I will never forget. "I want to tell you something," he began. His words sounded eerily familiar. "You should know that the situation you have experienced is very often fatal." And then, after a thoughtful pause, he concluded: "You are fortunate to be alive."

Once he learned of this ordeal, a good friend, Don Haymes, wrote to say that "God has given you back your life — now for the third time! — and once more reinforced . . . a radical sense of your contingency."[2] Don's words could not have hit home with any more

2. Letter from Don Haymes to Richard Hughes, December 21, 2000.

precision. I knew my life had been returned to me yet once again, and I felt profoundly grateful, but also more vulnerable than ever before. Don's words reinforced the truth that I already knew, that I am finite and completely contingent on a Power that transcends myself. This, of course, has been the fundamental argument of this book from its opening pages.

At the same time, I surely do not believe that God plays Russian roulette with human life, picking and choosing in arbitrary fashion who will live and who will die. One of the two cardiologists who cared for me at Bellin Hospital in Green Bay, Dr. Donald Jenny, perhaps put it best when he wrote in a personal letter,

> As a physician, I find clinical outcomes to be extremely inscrutable. . . . While there are many satisfying moments in my profession — and you are one of them — there are less fortunate outcomes in clinical situations that continue to be enigmatic for me as a physician: what is a miracle to one patient becomes an experience of sorrow and questioning by another.[3]

Now I must ask, what should I make of these life and death experiences, and how do they pertain to the themes of this book? How can they enhance the vocation of a Christian scholar? And how can they illumine answers to the question "How can Christian faith sustain the life of the mind?"

It seems clear today — six years after the heart attack and four years after the cancer and pulmonary emboli — that those events not only enhanced my sense of vocation; they helped *define* my sense of vocation in these closing years of my career. I am, after all, both a scholar and a Christian, and my encounters with the face of death brought both these callings into sharper focus.

I have been convinced, for example, of the reality of human fini-

3. Letter from Dr. Donald Jenny to Richard Hughes, February 23, 2001.

tude ever since my graduate student days at the University of Iowa. Today I understand the meaning of human finitude in fresh and compelling ways. Today I know in ways I did not before that human life is beset with radical limitations, that certainty lies in many respects beyond my grasp, and that I must therefore embrace genuine intellectual humility.

I have believed for many years that the theme of paradox is central to the gospel message. Today I understand that paradox more clearly. Thanks to my three encounters with the face of death, I know beyond a shadow of a doubt that my own life is incredibly fragile and can be lost in the blink of an eye. But I also know, in ways I did not before, that I am saved and redeemed, in spite of my sins and in spite of death's inevitability.

But in many respects, the most important lesson I learned came from the prompting of a friend who pointedly asked, "Since you have had your life returned to you on three different occasions, do you feel that God has a special work in store for you to do?" Frankly, I had resisted thinking in those terms, simply because the very question suggested that God had singled me out for special treatment — a conclusion that I reject.

My finitude means that I simply cannot know precisely when or where God works, how God works, or why. For example, a close friend of mine lost his struggle with pulmonary emboli some two years before I was spared. Am I to believe that God singled me out for life but singled my friend out for death? I am extraordinarily reluctant to make those kinds of claims.

Still, now that my friend had raised the issue of "a special work" for me to do, I determined to give that question some thought. I concluded that God does, indeed, have a special work for me to do, and that special work is simply to live a life of gratitude for the gift of life itself, and to translate that gratitude into acts of grace on behalf of those with whom I come in contact. Such a life is the vocation to which I have been called, both as a scholar and as a Christian.

Postscript to the Postscript

Sidney E. Mead, the historian of American religious history whose insights inspired chapter two of this book, was my teacher at the University of Iowa. Following my graduation from Iowa in 1971, Mead and I became good friends and carried on an extended correspondence for almost thirty years. I saw him occasionally, but those personal visits were all too infrequent. When I read *Tuesdays with Morrie*, I knew I had to see my old professor face to face at least one more time while he was still alive. After all, Mead had already lived to the ripe old age of 94 and, as it turned out, would pass away within a few short months on June 9, 1999, after a brief illness.

So I purchased an airline ticket and flew to Tucson, Arizona, where Mead and his wife Mildred were living in retirement. While I was there, I told Mead something that I had told him years ago, but something he had not fully grasped at the time. I told him that no two people had shaped my thinking more than he and Martin Luther, since he and Luther had taught me so much about what it means to be human.

After Mead had read *Tuesdays with Morrie*, he wrote a letter to me that contained the following lines:

> I may have been amazed, as you note, when you [linked me with Luther] some years ago. But now we have common terms with which to express it — you are saying that Luther and I each have "spent a lifetime 'musing [on] Tuesday's questions.'"[4]

And so I was. Martin Luther and Sidney Mead did, indeed, devote their lives to "Tuesday's questions," for "Tuesday's questions" are those questions each of us must ask when we ponder the meaning of our lives in the light of our inevitable deaths. Luther, the re-

---

4. Letter from Sidney E. Mead to Richard Hughes, October 1, 1998.

former, raised those questions with particular reference to personal guilt and condemnation. Mead, the man who devoted his academic career to understanding the American Enlightenment, raised those questions with particular reference to the meaning of human life in the United States and the meaning of the American experiment. Either way, by raising "Tuesday's questions," both Martin Luther and Sidney Mead sought to understand what it means to be a finite human being who stands before an infinite God.

The truth is, "Tuesday's questions" are those questions that every Christian scholar must ask time and again. If faithfully and honestly pursued, these are the questions that allow us to live and work in the midst of paradox. And precisely for that reason, these are the questions that allow Christian faith to sustain the life of the mind.